Equality
and Inclusion in
Early Childhood

2nd Edition

Jennie Lindon

HODDER
EDUCATION

Dedication

In loving memory of my father, the Celtic part of my heritage

Orders: please contact Bookpoint Ltd, 130 Milton Park, Abingdon, Oxon OX14 4SB.
Telephone: (44) 01235 827720. Fax: (44) 01235 400454. Lines are open from 9.00–5.00,
Monday to Saturday, with a 24-hour message answering service. You can also order through our website
www.hoddereducation.co.uk

British Library Cataloguing in Publication Data
A catalogue record for this title is available from the British Library

ISBN: 978 1 4441 4550 2

This Edition Published 2012
Impression number   10 9 8 7 6 5 4 3 2
Year   2015, 2014, 2013

Copyright © 2012 Jennie Lindon

Hachette UK's policy is to use papers that are natural, renewable and
recyclable products and made from wood grown in sustainable forests.
The logging and manufacturing processes are expected to conform to the
environmental regulations of the country of origin.

Cover photo © Jaimie Duplass – Fotolia

Typeset by DC Graphic Design Limited, Swanley Village, Kent.
Printed in Great Britain for Hodder Education, An Hachette UK Company, 338 Euston Road, London
NW1 3BH.

Contents

Introduction

In any book about childhood some general decisions need to be made about words. I use the non-specific term 'practitioner' to include the different kinds of professionals who take responsibility for children in early years provision, school and out-of-school facilities and the childminding service. It will be clear when I am talking about a particular type of provision. The word 'parents' covers anyone who takes the main family responsibility for children. Please assume the word always includes 'and other family carers'.

I have benefited from conversations over the years with many fellow professionals within the early years sector, college tutors and advisors and with a wide range of practitioners working directly with children. I have drawn from conversations with children as well as adults, and from my own observations, to develop fictional people and places for the scenarios in this book. In this revised, third edition, I was able to research using the extensive information now available on websites. However, I still appreciate the help I received via telephone or email on uncertain issues. All website addresses were correct at the time of writing (summer 2011). My thanks to Drew Lindon, who researched the online links.

Equality and Inclusion in Early Childhood covers a vital area of practice and one in which there will continue to be differences of opinion and interpretation. On especially contentious issues, my aim has been to make my position clear, with the rationale behind it. I have sought to distinguish between available information, for instance about law and guidance, and when I have expressed my professional viewpoint. Readers are responsible for seeking further information and advice if they face difficult decisions. This point is especially important if there are issues of interpretation of the law or related guidance. No section of this book claims to offer legal advice.

If I have made actual errors, then please let Hodder Education know and I will correct mistakes as soon as possible.

Equality for early childhood practice

Equality and inclusion are crucial practice issues for early years, school and playwork professionals. There are legal obligations around equality, but the moral responsibility is just as important. Babies are not born prejudiced or bigoted, yet children are enthusiastic learners – they imitate the words and actions of familiar adults and of other children. Rigid and divisive adult views can be reflected in children's choice of language, their expressed beliefs about groups in society, including their own sources of identity, and their choice of play companions.

Practitioners, of every background, share with children's families, from every social and ethnic group, the responsibility of raising the next generation with a strong sense of their self-worth, which does not depend on disrespect or disdain for other people. I think best practice with children should develop an outlook, summed up by Shami Chakrabarti, Director of Liberty, the human rights organisation, when interviewed for *The Times Magazine* (21 May 2011). She said:

'I'm anyone's equal but no one's superior.'

The main sections of this chapter cover:
- reflective practice
- equality and childhood.

Reflective practice

Young children are in the process of developing their attitudes, so early years, school and out-of-school practitioners are expected to be active in support of equality and inclusion. You are not expected to bring about changes in social circumstances beyond your control. However, within your professional sphere of influence, as a practitioner you have the responsibility to:
- Promote equality of opportunity equal chances – to the best of your ability for all children and families who are in contact with the service.
- Contribute to the development and running of early years provision that actively welcomes the wide range of children and families and addresses any barriers to inclusion.
- Work to equalise opportunities and reduce the impact of disadvantage for children and families whose situation or group identity could make them vulnerable.
- Foster respect and mutual understanding between children and families who see themselves as so different from each other that they do not expect to share

similar interests or concerns. Respect between groups is due in both directions. No group within the UK is excused from this obligation, regardless of whether they experience, or have experienced, inequalities within society.

- Extend your professional knowledge and understanding of equality and inclusion around gender, ethnic group, social and cultural background, faith and disability.

Working as a reflective practitioner

Good practice for equality is partly a focus on the individual children and families who attend your setting or service so that your work naturally reflects the immediate community and local environment. But good equality practice also covers the image of the world that you are giving children: the big picture that extends beyond their own backyard. You, as a practitioner, should not feel responsible for matters of inequality or discrimination outside your control. However, you are definitely responsible for what children learn while they are within your care in early years provision of any kind: school, out-of-school settings or your home as a childminder.

In nursery, after-school club or your own home as a childminder, you will often have to deal with tricky situations by making swift personal decisions about what to say and do, or whether to ignore an event. Continued professional development fosters the approach of being a reflective practitioner: someone who is willing and able to think over options and discuss with team or network colleagues. Equality in practice is definitely an area that benefits from some reflection, as outlined below.

- You need to be willing to acknowledge what you learned within your own childhood, as well as adulthood sources of your beliefs and assumptions.
- Discussion with team or network colleagues is important for airing ideas, sharing knowledge and, with support, addressing areas of practice that are less comfortable to face.
- Childminders, who usually work alone, need reflection and a chance to discuss issues, in order to be consistent over time in their reactions with children. If you work with an assistant or co-childminder, you need to discuss ways of handling sensitive situations.
- In group provision, it is essential that the whole staff team reaches an informed commitment over policy and, just as important, a shared understanding about what policy means in daily practice.
- There must be consistency between individual practitioners on key issues around how to handle types of situation that arise with children, in communication with parents or with fellow professionals.

Without a doubt, effective equality practice cannot stay with reflective discussion, however detailed, about getting the policy right or what might be done or said. Everyone needs to get to that point where something is actually said or done. For this reason, you will find sections in this book that offer direct suggestions. These examples are not telling you to use those actual words and nothing else; rather, my aim is to give you examples with which to work.

You will never be able to anticipate all possibilities. So professional practice has to be led by willingness to talk over situations that you have already handled. Sometimes you will need to inform a colleague about what you did or said. Sometimes you will welcome a chance to reflect on whether you could have taken a different route. Be kind to yourself; it is hard to think quickly when faced with a difficult situation. You can learn from reflection and be ready to take a different option next time.

Reflection on approaches to equality

Professional practice evolves and a grasp of social history is useful, if only to challenge any assumption that the current face of equality practice is completely right and will not change. At several points in this book I will need to be clear about my value stance. Now is one of those times.

- Good practice over equality does not mean blaming people for the past. A positive approach looks to the future. You are not responsible for what happened before you were even born. However, you are definitely responsible for your own attitudes now and your willingness, or resistance, about learning more and reflecting on your views.
- A culture of blame and attribution of guilt soured some approaches to anti-racist and anti-sexist initiatives during the 1980s. In some cases, blunt criticism of workshop delegates or accusatory behaviour set a negative, divisive model for how to address the issues and led to defensive reactions.
- Since that time, there has been a constructive shift to methods more likely to bring about reflection and change in outlook and actions. Effective challenge, rather than attack, leaves fellow professionals able to save face, find common ground and opt to change rather than focus on self-defence.

Action for equality should bring all groups on board in an even-handed way. Inclusive practice can never be about claiming that 'everyone is the same'; clearly they are not. Good practice rests upon ensuring that nobody is excluded, that children and families have equal chances to be acknowledged, respected and included in authentic ways. Existing social inequalities will mean that not all families have the same starting point. So broad intentions in equality practice need to be fine-tuned for the particular situation.

Equality practice for children needs to consider their current experiences. Children especially should not be expected to make up for past inequalities, or for those that still exist. They cannot be held responsible for the society into which they were born. But children can appreciate the impact now of their words and actions, and learn a more open approach than seemed possible for previous generations. Equality means everyone.

- Disabled children deserve to be treated as children first, and their child status brings responsibilities as well as rights. It is in nobody's interests if disabled children are excused fair boundaries for their behaviour.
- Girls need to show consideration to boys as well as vice versa, and a largely female workforce needs to take care in respecting boys' choices and preferences.
- Traveller or Gypsy children cannot be excused from offensive remarks to children from settled families because the latter do not belong to a defined minority ethnic group.
- Putting equality into practice is not a competitive exercise. Paying attention to one faith does not require pushing aside another. Celebrating Divali does not necessitate 'banning Christmas'.

Acknowledging differences should not entail judgement that one group or way of life is better than another. Different means just that – neither better nor worse. Within your practice all children, and their families, have the right to be treated with equal respect, attention and, when appropriate, concern for their well being.

The impact of adult attitudes on behaviour

All adults have developed attitudes about other people and the groups to which they belong. Attitudes are partly made up of feelings about other people or whole groups. But there is also an intellectual part that is formed by beliefs, expectations and assumptions. These are supported by information and the conviction that particular facts are true: the sense of 'everyone knows that ...'. You cannot see people's attitudes, but they become visible through behaviour: their actions and chosen words.

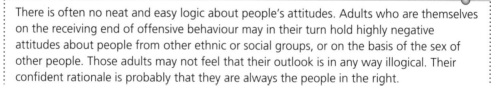

Take another **perspective**

There is often no neat and easy logic about people's attitudes. Adults who are themselves on the receiving end of offensive behaviour may in their turn hold highly negative attitudes about people from other ethnic or social groups, or on the basis of the sex of other people. Those adults may not feel that their outlook is in any way illogical. Their confident rationale is probably that they are always the people in the right.

Everyone holds attitudes. Some are mainly positive, some may be mildly rejecting of others, but some may be intensely offensive towards particular individuals, defined by gender, social class, faith or ethnic group. Attitudes are learned throughout childhood and some adults resist later change as emotionally challenging. Change is that much harder if someone's sense of self-worth depends strongly upon feeling superior to specific other people, defined as the 'wrong' sex, skin colour, faith, social class or other group marker. However, adults continue to learn and are potentially capable of rethinking their views and assumptions about others.

Figure 1.1 The world for young children is shaped by what adults make available

Stereotyping

Firm attitudes about other groups are usually supported by stereotypes. This word describes simple, relatively fixed, beliefs about the characteristics shared by individuals of an identified group.

- Stereotypes are usually unfavourable. For instance, 'Women are always so emotional,' 'Muslims are fanatical about their religion,' 'He's so irresponsible – typical working class.'
- Apparently complimentary stereotypes can have a serious sting in the tail when they restrict an individual's options to those that fit the stereotype. Examples would be, 'Disabled people are so brave' or 'Black boys are such natural athletes.'

Stereotypes are usually applied to groups to which the individuals speaking do not themselves belong. The development and maintenance of stereotypes depend on a belief that other groups have less variety than one's own.

- People are more ready to say of another social or ethnic group: 'They're all ...' or 'She's a typical ...'. But they will say of their own group: 'It all depends' or 'People differ, you can't say that about everybody.' Listen to daily conversations and you will notice this pattern.
- Stereotypes are often built from a particular event or experience, which is then generalised well beyond the original context of place and time. Firmly held stereotypes then shape the interpretation placed on experiences with individuals from the given group.

- People who appear to fit the stereotype are taken as further evidence of this person's beliefs. The experience of individuals who clearly do not fit is discounted as a reason to adjust beliefs because 'You're my friend, I don't count you' or 'Well, most of them aren't like her.'
- People who object to having stereotypes imposed upon them are frequently further labelled as 'touchy' or being the one who 'has a problem'.

Stereotypes are partly learned during childhood because children hear familiar adults, in the family or outside, expressing simplistic, fixed views about other people. Children remember these beliefs along with other information that they have gained from key adults in their lives. They repeat the beliefs unless experience leads them to question these views.

What does it mean?

Stereotypes: simplistic beliefs, which are resistant to change, about the characteristics allegedly shared by individuals of an identified group.

Stereotyping: the process of using such beliefs to shape expectations of individuals who belong, or are presumed to belong, to a given group, in order to predict or explain their actions.

Pause for reflection

Look at the examples that follow.

What kind of underlying beliefs are the speakers expressing? And what seems to be the source of their conviction that they are correct?

What might be the consequences if the comments go unchallenged? Silence from other adults will most likely be taken as agreement.

1 'Don't ask May's grandma to help the children on the computer. Older people aren't computer literate and she'll get all worried about it.'

2 'We let the boys run around and burn off their energy. There's no point in trying to make them sit and learn, they only fidget all the time.'

3 'Nur's parents shouldn't be trying to teach the child two languages at the same time. She should be learning English like everyone else. Nur can learn Turkish when she gets older and she's ready.'

4 'I don't care what you say. We'll never be able to work together with Prods. What on earth have we got in common with those Protestants?'

5 'Sunita looks a bit tired with the new baby, but she'll be fine. Asians always have extended families, don't they? There'll be loads of aunties helping out.'

6 'I'll wait until Liam's mother comes in tomorrow. His father has this dreadful stammer and any conversation takes for ever. It's so embarrassing and I don't think he understands half of what I say.'

7 'I'm really not sure about asking Isaac's father about the Hanukkah celebrations. Jewish people are so touchy, aren't they? Don't you remember Rebecca's mother?'

8 'I give the children a proper balanced diet here, none of this vegetarian nonsense. They need to have a normal diet when they're little; they can choose for themselves when they get older.'

9 'We've got some children coming on a visit to the country. I bet none of them has seen a cow before, let alone walked up a hill. These inner-city families never take their children anywhere.'

Language reflects attitudes

Attitudes are represented through choice of words and phrases, even when adults are not conscious of the implications of what they say. Words matter because they are a reflection of deeply entrenched attitudes in our society.

- Historically there have been more negative associations with the colour/shade of black than white. The whole 'Black is beautiful' movement originating in the United States from the 1960s was a concerted attempt to reclaim the word and create positive associations.

- People who avoid racist remarks based directly on skin colour still sometimes use, perhaps without thinking, other offensive phrases, such as 'acting Jewish' (an implication of meanness) or 'Welshing on a deal' (untrustworthiness).

- There is a range of insults based on a negative view of being female: 'fussing like an old woman'; or upset boys are criticised for 'acting just like a girl'. Some spoken and written examples still use a generic 'he' to cover both sexes, or terms like 'mankind', when the discussion is about everyone.

- Words like 'cripple' or 'spastic' are used less often now as general insults. But you will notice comments like 'He's deaf as a post' or 'You blind or something?!' used to criticise someone for general inattention.

- The word 'gay' has been around for a long time, although with some very different meanings. In the Victorian era, the word was used to describe a racy, louche lifestyle for men. For much of the 20th century the word meant lively and fun loving. In the last decades of that century, support organisations for homosexual men claimed the word as a positive description for themselves. Following from that change, 'gay' also became a generalised playground insult between some children and adolescents.

Changing the words people use does not magically change their attitudes. However, an awareness of your use of words is a valuable part of a more general willingness to consider your attitudes. Unquestioned habits of language also extend to beliefs about those groups about which it is considered fine to make jokes.

In mainland Britain there has been a tradition of 'Irish jokes', in which the punchline depends on a belief that Irish people are stupid. Similar patterns can be found in other countries, except that the targeted ethnic or national group varies. For example, in the United States this kind of barbed witticism has been known as the 'Polish joke' and in Scandinavia it is the 'Norwegian joke'. Traditionally, members of the given ethnic group can choose to tell such jokes. The longest run of 'Irish jokes' I have ever heard was during a convivial post-conference evening with the delegation from Belfast (and they did regard themselves as Irish; see page 66).

Take another **perspective**

Previous generations in Britain expressed a casual anti-Semitism and disdain of 'foreigners', and the associated language became part of ordinary conversation. Try some Agatha Christie books written in the 1920s or 1930s. You will soon notice that the heroes and heroines – not the villains – use what reads now as anti-Semitism and dismissive terms for anyone who is not British. In terms of stereotyping, some decent minor characters from such groups are allowed to be an exception.

Attitudes about foreigners and Black ethnic groups also affected books written for children. The views were very clear in children's comics well up to the 1960s and early 1970s. Adults may not regard comics as real literature, but children read them with great enthusiasm.

Words matter – but so does courtesy

Responsible practitioners are observant of reactions to their spoken language and adjust in the light of feedback, even if they had no intention of being impolite or operating to exclude. However, it is important to avoid getting stuck in endless debates over words as an alternative to useful action. During the 1980s an initially constructive examination of use of words and phrases became weighed down by arguments about terminology. Some of the wilder, newsworthy stories about political correctness were myth; others were only slightly exaggerated.

Offhand or thoughtless language needs to be picked up, but in ways that still leave anyone – children, young people or fellow adults – with the ability to save face and make a choice to change for the future (see pages 127 or 129). Offensive language, in a context when it seems clear that insult was intended, needs to be challenged – whatever the group identity of the person who expressed this view. Otherwise, it is disruptive to behave as if there are 'right' and 'wrong' words in absolute terms. Equality and good relations between different groups are not promoted when well-intentioned practitioners, or other people, are criticised solely for their choice of words.

Knowledge of social history over equality issues soon tells you that preferred words or phrases change. Some people are left with 'out-of-date' phrases that they continue to use with courteous, not offensive, intentions. The older White generation in the UK population was taught that 'coloured' was the polite way to refer to anyone not of White appearance. Some people still use 'mentally handicapped' as the courteous term and will not have heard the phrase 'learning disabilities'.

Furthermore, at any one time you will find arguments between specialists within the equality field about 'correct' terminology.

EQUALITY AND INCLUSION IN EARLY CHILDHOOD

Over the years of the different editions of this book, there have been impassioned arguments over whether it should be 'disabled children' or 'children with disabilities'. That war over words was put to rest most effectively by parents who said sharply that the exact phrase used to describe their children was considerably less important than doing something effective to help.

When I wrote the first edition, some race equality specialists were adamant that the travelling community should not be called gypsies, because that was a term of insult, probably racist. However, this stance had disappeared by the time of the second edition. A distinct group within the travelling community called themselves Gypsies and made their views crystal clear (page 56).

A well-rounded diversity model for equality and inclusion works on the assumption that most people mean well most of the time – certainly unless there is clear evidence to the contrary. Practitioners in any of the professions involved with children and families cannot work to make a difference for equality and inclusion if they are highly anxious about using the wrong word or phrase. It is not acceptable professional behaviour for anyone to boost their sense of worthiness by getting on a verbal high horse about terms: accusing others of racism, sexism and various other -isms.

Key words and phrases

Writers and advisors, with equivalent commitment and experience, do not all agree on the exact meaning for key terms within equality practice. There follows a list of the definitions I have used in this book and these reflect some changes since the last edition. There is further discussion about terms on page 25 in the context of the Equality Act 2010.

General terms

Equality practice: a move towards the common ground for different group identities of promoting equality in an active way and dealing with issues that undermine equality or operate in a discriminatory way.

Promoting equality/equal opportunities/equal chances: actions integral to regular practice in order to ensure that all children are enabled to have positive experiences supporting personal identity. Action is taken if children's opportunities are blocked in ways that practitioners can directly address.

Anti-discriminatory practice (ADP): an active attempt to promote positive attitudes and behaviour, to challenge and change negative outlooks and actions, on the basis of any group identity. This approach stresses that practitioners should take the initiative, rather than be passive and wait until there is no option but to do something.

Anti-bias practice: a deliberate approach to play experiences and resources that avoids stereotypes and actively promotes understanding and knowledge of all groups within society.

Inclusion: this term, along with an inclusive approach, was initially developed with reference to disability. This term, and *social inclusion* now refer to general practice about equality. The terms mean an active effort to address ways in which children or adults may be excluded from services or experiences, whether this result was intentional or the result of unreflective practice. *Inclusion* is still used sometimes to refer specifically to equality issues over disability.

Race and racial equality

Race: the word used within equality practice to cover a group of people defined by their race (if that makes sense to them), skin colour, ethnic or national origins.

Racial equality: this phrase is used to describe promoting equal opportunities and challenging discrimination on the basis of racial/ethnic group as defined by legislation (see page 23).

Racism: the set of attitudes, actions and practice that subordinates a group of people because of their skin colour, culture or ethnic group. Racist beliefs are used to justify racial discrimination – the denial or restriction of opportunities to individuals from the defined group.

Ethnicity and ethnic group identity

Ethnic group: a grouping of people with a shared heritage of customs, language and possibly faith. People within a group have their national or cultural origins in common.

Minority ethnic group: an ethnic group with a relatively small number of individuals, in comparison with the national population. The group might nevertheless comprise the majority within a particular neighbourhood.

Black and Minority Ethnic (BME): a term that has emerged since the first edition of this book. The phrase is used to cover people visibly identified by a darker skin colour whose ethnic group identity is Caribbean, African or Asian. There is no agreed equivalent to describe people in UK society not covered by Black and Minority Ethnic. The census categories are a possible source of ideas. The options given to people who would classify themselves as White are appropriately wide. On this basis I have used White and Black as very general terms in this book when the point being made is that general.

If you want to find out more

- Commission for Racial Equality, undated but post 2001, *Ethnic Monitoring: a Guide for Public Authorities,* **www.equalityhumanrights.com/uploaded_files/PSD/12_ ethnic_monitoring.pdf**

Culture and cultural identity

Culture: describes the particular patterns of behaviour and associated beliefs that are shared by the individuals within a given group. Not all individuals will necessarily follow these patterns in exactly the same way. The term *cultural identity* is sometimes used instead of *national identity*.

Cultural diversity: the sense that a society includes myriad cultural sources and people who locate their identity in different cultural backgrounds. There is usually a great deal of within-group variation as well as broad differences and overlap between groups.

Multicultural: a word to describe a society, like that of the UK, in which the population is drawn from many distinct cultural backgrounds. The word is often misapplied, rather like 'ethnic', to mean not White European.

Faiths and religious belief

Faith or religion: a set of beliefs and practices built around one or more deities or individuals with paranormal powers.

Sects: the subdivisions that have formed within most world faiths after disagreements over detail of belief or religious practice.

Religious intolerance: hostility expressed by members of one faith towards a different faith, or between those who hold to a faith and people who do not follow any religious faith.

Anti-Semitism: religious intolerance and discrimination targeted at people of the Jewish faith and/or cultural background.

Sectarianism: intolerance expressed towards members of another denomination of the same religious faith. This form of discrimination can occur at an individual, group, cultural and institutional level.

Anti-sectarianism: the active attempt to challenge bigotry and inequalities that arise from a sectarian outlook and from religious intolerance of other types.

Sex and gender

Sex and sex differences: refer to the biological differences, created by the genes when babies are conceived, between boys and girls, men and women.

Gender: describes the psychological identity of being male or female, and the awareness of what sex differences mean within the social context.

Gender equality: aims and practice to promote equalising of opportunities on the basis of sex. Some writers prefer 'gender equity'.

Gender stereotypes: firm beliefs about the characteristics, behaviour, talents or weaknesses of individuals on the basis of their male or female identity.

Sexism: an outlook of prejudiced attitudes and discriminatory behaviour towards individuals on the basis of their sex.

Sexual orientation: the preference about sex of partner made by young people or adults: for the opposite sex, their own sex or both sexes.

Disability

Disabled children or children with disabilities: children who live with any kind of continuing sensory impairment or chronic health condition that affects their development and/or daily life.

Children with special needs: the same meaning as disabled children. The phrase can be unclear, since all children have individual wishes and specific needs. The phrase originally included gifted children, but in practice has been applied to disability and chronic ill health.

Equality and childhood

A thorough understanding of how children learn has to underpin best practice for equality. During early childhood, children learn an impressive range of skills and a large body of knowledge. By middle childhood, they still have a great deal to learn, but they already have a firm basis to their view of the world. They have developed, and will continue to develop, their social attitudes about other children and people in general. By four or five years of age, children have developed opinions about and expectations of others, whom they judge to be like them or unfamiliar from what they already know. Children have also established views, which are still open to change, about their place in their social world, their personal identity and sense of self-worth.

Awareness of differences

Children are visually curious; they look at and are interested in people and the events around them. As they learn to talk, children comment out loud on what has caught their interest. What young children say will depend on their experiences so far, based mainly on their neighbourhood and family.

Four- and five-year-olds tend to remark on physical differences and contrasts with children or adults who do not fit their experience so far. They notice and often share their observations with familiar adults, with the assumption that you will be interested, too. Sometimes what children have seen or heard leads them to ask a question, but not always.

- Children may point out an adult who is strikingly tall or heavy in comparison with the adults in their social network. They may comment, 'That lady looks awfully old' or 'Why is that man so little?' Part of adult responsibility is to explain courteously to a child that their comments may be accurate but concern for other people's feelings means that observations should be made at less than top volume.
- Children are learning about boys and girls, and their observation of differences is often linked with trying to sort out what makes someone a girl or a boy. They

may comment about another child, 'Is Nula really a girl? She's got very short hair.'

- As children encounter disabled peers or adults, they are likely to comment. A young child may say, 'Did you know that Andy in my playgroup has a thing to make his ears work?' or 'Marsha's daddy sits in a big buggy. Now why does he do that?'
- In a diverse neighbourhood, children may remark that some of their play companions are different in skin colour from themselves. Many parts of the UK have some level of ethnic group diversity, but the variation is not reflected in skin colour. So young children may make an accurate observation that seeing a child with a dark skin colour is unusual or that an adult is dressed in an unfamiliar way.

Figure 1.2 Childhood is a time of busy learning – about everything

Change and stability

Adults who pay close attention to what children say and to their questions can learn a great deal about the development of children's thinking, as well as their current knowledge. The observations of parents and practitioners may be a source of endearing stories about children, but they are also a window onto children's emotional and intellectual world.

One area of children's learning focuses on what changes and what does not. Children observe that other people differ in many respects, but they are working out which physical characteristics will change as they grow older. Children are initially grounded in the present and what they personally know. So it can be a revelation to a boy that he will not always be a child; one day he will be a man, rather like his daddy, but he will not be able to become a mummy. In a similar way, children are often surprised to realise, perhaps by looking in the family photograph album, that Grandma was once a young person, even a child.

When children realise that some features change, they begin to wonder whether everything can change. They have to learn about those characteristics that are stable throughout life. So it is not surprising if some children allow for the possibility that their sex or skin colour, or that of their friends, might change as they get older or because of circumstances. Children are learning about health, illness and disability and it is not obvious to them which are the conditions from which people can recover. So a child might reasonably ask, 'When will Andy's ears get better?' You may explain to a child that comments about people are usually best made in a quieter voice. It is a different situation from calling out, 'Hey, look at the big, yellow lorry!' because lorries do not have feelings.

From awareness to prejudice

Children who notice physical differences do not immediately assume that some characteristics are more valued. However, they are able to learn negative attitudes with the same ease that they are learning so many other ideas in their young lives. Children will use the prejudiced words and actions of adults, or other children, to build negative images of people from a given faith or ethnic group, or people with visible disabilities. Attitudes of rejection can limit children's choice of friends and show in their words and behaviour towards children, or adults, from the defined group which they have learned to dismiss.

Children who live in divided communities learn the religious or social distinctions that are important to local adults, even when outsiders would be hard pressed to distinguish between the groups. Some writers focus on how anti-Muslim feeling has been absorbed by children over the early years of the 21st century (Lane and Baig, 2003). However, more than one generation of children has grown up with the conflict in Northern Ireland. Honest observation and research have documented the ease with which young children learn the bigotry that supports sectarianism. They become alert to symbols, such as flags or choice of sports, used to tell Catholic from Protestant (Connolly et al., 2002). Sectarianism is also a serious issue in some parts of Scotland.

Children's personal identity

Young children steadily develop a sense of themselves as a unique person. Their personal identity builds from many aspects:

- Their own name and an understanding of whether they are a girl or a boy.
- Their immediate family, and their place in relation to their parents, brothers and sisters and other close relatives.
- How they look and how people react to their looks.
- What they can do and what they cannot do, and whether this seems to matter to other people.

- A growing sense of 'what we do in my family' – children's experience of cultural tradition and religious faith or other significant beliefs within their daily lives.

Children's sense of identity and of self-esteem will depend a great deal on their experience of other people – children and adults – and their social world. Children may feel mainly positive about themselves, that they are worthwhile individuals and valued by others. Or they may doubt themselves and wonder whether some of the sources of their personal identity, perhaps being a girl or having a visible disability, make them less worthy than other children. All children have the right to feel confident that their ethnic group and cultural background are valuable and of potential interest to their peers, as well as to people who share the same or a very similar background.

Mixed heritage

Men and women have married, or formed long-standing partnerships, across every social, ethnic, faith and other group boundary. Personal commitments have been made in communities where such behaviour provokes disapproval, rejection and violence, even when the union has been illegal. Children's identity is, then, potentially a blend of their heritage from both parents. Adults aware of racist attitudes in society have sometimes taken the view that children with two parents of different skin colour must commit to one side or the other: that they have to be either White or Black. Children from inter-faith relationships are sometimes given a similar stark choice.

Increasingly, it seems that children and young people are standing firm to determine their own identity, and that can include an insistence on valuing all sources of their family heritage. Studies of parents in mixed-race and mixed-faith families (Caballero et al., 2008; Parker and Song, 2001) show that individual families take a range of approaches. A key issue is that professionals do not make assumptions about the dynamics of mixed families, or what will, or will not, be best for the children.

In the UK, a considerable number of couples bridge various ethnic, social and faith group boundaries. Some live with the full support of their extended family and community, but not all. External pressures can be very strong on families, and some fragment under the strain. Children of mixed ethnic group parentage are over-represented in the population of looked-after children (those who have become the responsibility of their local authority), as are children of inter-faith couples in Northern Ireland.

There is not full agreement about a general term for children or adults whose family background brings together two or more ethnic group backgrounds. Phrases include 'mixed parentage', 'dual heritage' and 'multiple heritage'. If you need to know about individuals, invite them to self-describe. For some years, when parents differed by race or skin colour, the term 'mixed race' was unacceptable to professionals working in equality because of problems with the word 'race'. Oddly, 'race equality' remained acceptable over that time. Since the second edition of this book, it has become more acceptable, professionally, to use the phrase 'mixed race' (Houston, 2007; Parker and Song, 2001). The change in attitude seems to be due, at least in part, to a conviction that 'race' as a pseudo-scientific term has been effectively quashed.

Positive pride rather than superiority

Children deserve a sense of pride in their sources of personal identity, but it is unjust if they achieve their confidence at the cost of other children's self-esteem. Some children learn to boost their sense of self-worth by being disdainful about a child of the opposite sex, rude about a disabled child or rejecting of a child from an ethnic group different from their own.

This pattern can be learned through childhood from the family. Adults who experience a socially deprived position in life can be especially vulnerable to building an identity mainly through disparaging other social or ethnic groups. This pattern is not exclusive to White ethnic groups. Children may hear adults who are keen to blame another group for their misfortunes. In an economically hard-pressed neighbourhood, one group may be convinced that other people have gained unfair advantages. Offensive attitudes are not, of course, restricted to those families with few sources of positive identity. People with no financial worries and a secure social position can be breathtakingly dismissive of others not in their social class or ethnic group.

Young children develop attitudes

Some adults are still resistant to considering equality issues as they apply to childhood, especially early childhood. This resistance is reflected in the most ill-informed newspaper stories about equality practice. Some adults claim that children are 'innocent' and do not notice social or ethnic group differences, so they cannot develop attitudes based on such visible differences. But how could children not notice and learn? Adults responsible for young children base much of their everyday contact on the belief that children are alert to their surroundings and that they learn from what they hear and see.

Adults may prefer to believe children do not notice those aspects of the world that the adults themselves would rather remained outside children's experience. Adults are especially uneasy if they believe that noticing a difference is the same as saying the difference matters and makes some people better than others.

- Many adults, and that still includes some practitioners, believe that if you say that children notice ethnic group differences, such as skin colour, then you must also be saying that the children are prejudiced. This is not the case.
- Adults can no longer easily distinguish awareness and prejudice; children are still learning. In a similar way, a child who notices another child's disability is not automatically being offensive about that individual, or about disability in general. It depends so much on what is said and in what way.

Another source of adult unease arises from lack of confidence about how to react when children express curiosity, display potential prejudices about others or show distress at offence aimed at them. It feels easier to take the approach that alert and curious children do not notice any of the visible differences of sex, ethnic group or disability.

For a long time, many practitioners claimed that, since they never touched upon social or ethnic group differences, they could not possibly exert any influence over children's developing attitudes. This approach was sometimes linked with the claim that talking about such topics destroys childhood 'innocence'.

- Even limited observation of children soon shows that they do not just learn what adults intend them to learn through deliberate telling or showing.
- Children are busy building their attitudes from what they see in their immediate play environment and, by implication, from what is absent.
- They learn from what adults say, but also from topics of conversation that adults avoid or with which they look uncomfortable.

Treating children with equality does not mean treating them all the same. This mistaken approach muddles up fair treatment of young children with behaving as if they lack individuality. Children are not all the same and it is poor practice to pretend that they are. Adults are being dishonest if they claim not to notice the ethnic group, sex or ability differences that make children into unique individuals. Reflective and good practice over equality is to work out in what ways it is appropriate to treat children as different, but with equal attention and respect offered to all children and their families.

As equality practice has become an integral part of best early years practice, another issue has emerged that merits just as much attention. One conceptual strand on equality issues applies analysis of social power to the world of childhood. The argument is that long-standing inequalities in our society, especially of race and sex, mean that some patterns of behaviour, even of young children, should be judged as more reprehensible than others. Examples of this approach can be found in David Gillborn on race equality (2008) and Naima Browne (2004) on gender. In my view, the serious problem with this approach is that it lays an unjustified responsibility on children, as young as early childhood, for the actions and inactions of older generations. As children themselves could say, 'It is just so unfair.'

Pause for reflection

- Be honest with yourself and also, if you are a manager, about your staff team. Do some of the views described above influence your practice?
- Are children seen sometimes as 'innocent' or 'unaware' in an unrealistic way?
- What are the consequences for children if their reactions and actions are judged against inequalities in the adult social world?

- Are some adult comments or reactions a way of stepping aside from a fuller discussion about what is going on between the children?
- Could any of these adult outlooks in action have the consequences of blocking children's experience or their developing sense of self-worth?

If you want to find out more

- Baldock, P. (2010) *Understanding Cultural Diversity in the Early Years*. London: Sage.
- Browne, N. (2004) *Gender Equity in the Early Years*. Maidenhead: Open University Press.
- Caballero, C., Edwards, R. and Puthussery, S. (2008) *Parenting 'Mixed' Children: Differences and Belonging in Mixed Race and Faith Families*. Joseph Rowntree Foundation, **www.jrf.org.uk/publications/parenting-mixed-children-difference-and-belonging**
- Connolly, P., Smith, A. and Kelly, B. (2002) *Too Young to Notice: the Cultural and Political Awareness of 3–6 year olds in Northern Ireland*. Belfast: Community Relations Council.
- CPIS, *Children's Play Information Service*, **www.ncb.org.uk/cpis (accessed 27 July 2011).**
- Early Years Equality (EYE), 'Multi-strand equality issues with a primary focus on race', **www.earlyyearsequality.co.uk** (accessed 27 July 2011).
- Equality and Human Rights Commission, *Glossary of Terms*, **www.equalityhumanrights.com/**
- Gillborn, D. (2008) *Racism and Education: Coincidence or Conspiracy?* London: Routledge.
- Houston, G. (2007) *Mixed Race, Not Mixed Up!* Wallasey: Early Years Equality.
- Johnson, P. and Kossykh, Y. (2008) *Early Years, Life Chances and Equality: A Literature Review*. Manchester: Equality and Human Rights Commission, **www.equalityhumanrights.com/uploaded_files/research/7_earlyyears_lifechances.pdf**
- Joseph Rowntree Trust, **www.jrf.org.uk/publications**
- Lane, J. and Baig, R. (2003) *Building Bridges for Our Future: The Way Forward through Times of Terror and War*. Wallasey: Early Years Equality.
- Learning and Teaching Scotland, **www.ltscotland.org.uk**
- Lindon, J. (2010), *Reflective Practice and Early Years Professionalism*. London: Hodder Education.
- Parker, D. and Song, M. (eds) (2001) *Rethinking 'Mixed Race'*. London: Pluto Press.
- The Runnymede Trust, **www.runnymedetrust.org/**

Equality law, guidance and policy

Professional practice requires a grasp of the main laws within the UK that relate to equality. This chapter describes, in brief, how legislation affects work with children and families. It is your professional responsibility, especially for team leaders or advisors, to know how to find out more. However, you need to seek proper legal advice if you face a challenge based on requirements by law.

The main sections of this chapter cover:
- equality in law
- policy for equality.

Equality in law

Legislation does not automatically change behaviour or attitudes, but laws make a public statement about what is acceptable or unacceptable within a given society. Good practice for equality and inclusion is considerably broader than the requirements of the law described in this chapter. There are moral issues around what you judge to be the right way to deal with daily situations. All the fine details of legislation will not cover everything in your practice. The law, however, places a crucial framework around what you do in your professional life with children and families.

Where laws apply

Laws create a framework for residents of the UK by defining some boundaries around what must or must not be done. The UK comprises four nations: England, Wales, Scotland and Northern Ireland. The central government determines some legislation that applies across the UK and passes through Parliament at Westminster, London. Historically, Scotland has operated with a high level of self determination and can set legislation through the Scottish Parliament in Edinburgh. The Northern Ireland Assembly, in Belfast, can make laws for the Province. The process of devolution did not give Wales the power to make laws. However, the National Assembly for Wales, in Cardiff, exercises considerable control over how legislation is put into practice and the shape of services for this nation within the UK.

You will first hear about possible laws when they are debated in Parliament or Assembly. Proposed primary legislation is usually known as a Bill. When it has passed to become law, the legislation tends to be known as an Act in England,

Wales and Scotland, and an Order in Northern Ireland. You will often hear or read about Bills that are in process, so it is important to recall that proposed sections often get modified during the debate. Some proposed Bills are defeated and do not become law – at least not this time around.

Law, guidance and advice

The legislation described in this chapter is primary legislation and the requirements built into the laws must be obeyed. However, legal language is not expressed in a way that allows straightforward application to daily life.

In the years after any new law has been passed, there are often court cases that test sections that are open to more than one interpretation. Legal decisions following this challenge build a resource called case law. This information sets definite precedents for when a similar disagreement arises in the future. You may see case law quoted in newspapers or information leaflets in the format of 'Green versus Bloggs' or 'Bloggs versus the Crown'.

Sometimes the relevant government department issues further information through books of guidance or codes of practice. These documents do not have the same force as primary legislation, but they are described as statutory. Sometimes this statutory guidance is called a Code of Practice. It is required that

Figure 2.1 In what kind of society do you want them to grow up?

EQUALITY AND INCLUSION IN EARLY CHILDHOOD

local authorities or relevant organisations follow the details of statutory guidance or a code. Some good practice guidance is recommended, meaning that the associated government department strongly advises that the suggestions and examples are followed. These distinctions matter because it is not good professional practice to tell others that something is 'the law' or 'we are legally obliged to…' when that statement is untrue.

What does it mean?

Primary legislation: the term used for laws that have been passed for a given country. The detail of law defines what is legally required or has been made illegal. The name of a law is given, with the date that it was passed by Parliament or Assembly.

Statutory guidance: issued by the relevant government department to explain some laws in less-legal language. Such guidance, often called a Code of Practice, describes what must be done or not done.

Good practice guidance: often issued to support professionals and organisations to put law and statutory guidance into daily practice. These publications may be 'recommended' by the relevant government department or 'commended' in a foreword by a minister.

Case law: built through court cases when individuals or organisations challenge the interpretation of a law. The legal decision at the end of the case establishes a precedent that can be used in the future.

This section now describes the key concepts within legislation for equality and the main provisions of the laws. This information is correct to the best of my understanding, from the resources given on page 22. At no point does this chapter offer legal advice, especially if any readers face a complex decision, for instance over staffing, that rests on interpretation of legal requirements.

The Equality Act 2010

Legislation relevant to equality was initially most concerned with identifying discriminatory actions and making them unlawful. Over the final decades of the 20th century there was a significant shift towards legislation that also established an active duty to promote equality and equal treatment. Since the 1970s, laws came onto the statute books to address separate areas of equality and discrimination.

Legislation applies to all residents of the country, including children, unless a specific exclusion has been made. Respect for different cultural traditions, or a strongly held belief, never overrules the law; any exceptions have to be specified. Everyone who lives in the UK is subject to existing legislation.

The Equality Act 2010 came into force in 2011 for England, Wales and Scotland. This law brought together the existing separate laws to harmonise legislation within a single framework for equality. The Equality Act 2010 has created the Commission for Equality and Human Rights. The CEHR is the regulatory body to ensure equality, human rights and anti-discrimination within England, Wales and Scotland.

Northern Ireland

Apart from a few minor exceptions, The Equality Act 2010 does not apply to Northern Ireland. At the time of writing, this part of the UK does not have a single law for equality; legislation continues to address the separate areas.

The Equality Commission for Northern Ireland is the regulatory body for this part of the UK. The Commission oversees the implementation of key legislation on sex discrimination, race equality and disability. The Commission is also pressing for legislative reform to close the gaps in law for equality between Northern Ireland and the rest of the UK.

The Race Relations (NI) Order 1997 addresses race equality in Northern Ireland and the Order specifically included the Irish Traveller community as a racial group. Sex equality is addressed by the Sex Discrimination (Northern Ireland) Order 1976. The Equality (Disability etc.) (Northern Ireland) Order 2000 expanded the duties and powers of the Equality Commission to be much more active in promoting equalisation of opportunities for disabled people in Northern Ireland. The Special Educational Needs and Disability Order 2005 (SENDO) aimed to give full rights to mainstream education for disabled children.

In Northern Ireland, religious affiliation has divided Protestant and Catholic Christians. The Fair Employment and Treatment (Northern Ireland) Order 1998 requires organisations to avoid direct or indirect discrimination and victimisation on the basis of religious or political affiliation, or supposed affiliation. Legal requirements exist for monitoring job recruitment by religious (or community) affiliation and the possibility of affirmative action.

If you want to find out more

- ACAS (2010) *Rights at Work: Equality and Discrimination,* www.acas.org.uk/media/pdf/a/3/Equality___discrimination(RAW)_OCTOBER_2010.pdf
- Age UK, www.ageuk.org.uk/work-and-learning/discrimination-and-rights/default-retirement-age---frequently-asked-questions
- Equality and Human Rights Commission (EHRC) *Glossary of Terms* and *Protected Characteristics,* also other information pages, www.equalityhumanrights.com (accessed 1 September 2011).
- Equality Commission for Northern Ireland, *The Gaps between GB and NI Equality Law,* www.equalityni.org (accessed 1 September 2011).

Protected characteristics

The Equality Act 2010 has established a list of nine 'protected characteristics'. These specify the grounds on which it is unlawful to discriminate. The characteristics are:

Age – specific age of an adult. Children are excluded from the age discrimination aspect, on the grounds that their inclusion would have made it difficult to treat them appropriately on the basis of their age.

Disability – physical or mental impairment which has a substantial and long-term adverse effect on this person's life.

Gender reassignment – the process of transitioning from one gender to another.

Marriage between a man and a woman, and civil partnership between same-sex couples

Pregnancy and maternity.

Race – a group of people defined by their race, colour and nationality (including citizenship), ethnic or national origin.

Religion or belief – faith within organised religion, but also any set of philosophical beliefs that influences how someone lives their life. So atheism is included. Previous law on race equality did not cover faith. Some groups – Jews, Sikhs and Travellers or Gypsies were covered on the basis of shared ethnic group identity, whereas Muslims were not covered by the previous law, because Islam is a faith followed by people from many different ethnic groups.

Sex – being male or female.

Sexual orientation – whether a person's sexual attraction is to their own sex, the opposite sex or to both sexes.

Some of these protected characteristics are directly relevant to close relationships with children in the course of early years practice. Other characteristics are relevant to your working relationships with parents and other family carers, within the staff group and the process of recruitment to the team, or in other professional relationships. The protected characteristic of age is relevant for recruitment of new staff and also for exiting staff, because there is no longer a national default retirement age (DRA: an age at which employers can insist that staff stop work). Age alone cannot be a basis for deciding that someone is unable to fulfil the responsibilities of a post.

Taking reasonable steps

The broad legal obligation is to avoid discriminatory practice on the basis of any of the protected characteristics. The obligation is to remove disadvantage by taking what is called 'all reasonable steps'. The word 'reasonable' arises frequently in descriptions of what is expected for anyone to remain within the law. The point is that people are expected to address those issues which are within their control. Their actions should be 'proportionate' to the situation – appropriate, necessary and possible for them to undertake.

In terms of staff, or potential staff, managers (and any other bodies involved in recruitment) are obligated to make 'reasonable adjustments', for example to respect the beliefs of a colleague. However, it is still necessary that any staff member can fulfil the obligations of the job. Strongly held beliefs are not an open-ended right to decline key parts of the job description.

Responsible managers have regard to the demands of the job. Taking good care of babies, toddlers and young children requires a reasonable state of fitness and mobility in staff. Proportionate adjustments can be appropriate for disabled colleagues or practitioners who are pregnant. However, the concept of protected characteristics does not enable staff, or potential staff, to rewrite their role. They cannot demand to continue in their job despite the reality that their physical or mental impairment means they cannot guarantee the safety and well being of children in their charge.

Active promotion of equality

Over the decades, new equality legislation has increasingly gone beyond a legal requirement to avoid discriminatory behaviour. The legal obligation includes an active response to ensure equality and equal chances. This requirement is part of the Equality Act 2010, but the details are yet to emerge in full. The relevant laws and guidance in Northern Ireland also encompass this proactive approach.

The principle continues, which was established with earlier disability equality legislation, that service providers should make reasonable adjustments in anticipation of the diversity of service users. For example, a nursery should have considered ease of access before a child or parent in a wheelchair arrives at the door. Issues over mobility and ease of access affect a noticeable proportion of the population; it is fair to expect any service to be ready.

Previous legislation for race equality required a more proactive role for any public bodies, including early years provision and education, to work towards racial equality. Settings were required to monitor how their services were used and outcomes for ethnic groups. This requirement meant, for instance, that schools have had to establish ethnic group monitoring of the academic achievements of pupils and patterns of school exclusion rates. Information needs to show whether there are significant differences by ethnic group identity. The school would then have to explore the reasons for the differences, and take effective and appropriate action to resolve the anomaly.

The Equality Act 2010 introduced a Public Sector Equality Duty that local authorities should have due regard to eliminated unlawful discrimination but also fostering good relations across all the areas of equality and advancing equality of opportunity. The Equality Act was implemented within the last weeks of the Labour government. The Coalition government at Westminster halted the implementation of the regulations relevant to this duty. At the time of writing (summer 2011), the revised version has not yet emerged. So new codes of practice are not yet available.

Key concepts within equality legislation

The following terms are used regularly within the legal framework for equality. Any legal challenge against behaviour would have to demonstrate that action, or inaction, was unlawful. Defence or justification would have to show that there were sound, non-discriminatory reasons for the behaviour.

Affirmative action: positive steps taken to increase the participation of any groups which are currently under-represented in the workplace. Any steps must be consistent with guidance about what is, or is not, acceptable to promote increased participation.

Direct discrimination – rejecting or favouring someone, for instance for a service or employment, on the basis of their group identity, the protected characteristic in the Equality Act 2010. The motive for such behaviour is irrelevant; what matters is the discriminatory result.

Harassment – behaving towards people in a consistently hostile way, so as to create an intimidating or hostile environment for them. The Equality Act created a legal responsibility for employers to their staff over harassment by third parties. In early years provision, that would mean that the nursery manager is obliged to take reasonably practicable steps to prevent the harassment of a practitioner by a colleague or a parent. However, the Coalition government has committed to modify or remove this requirement. At the time of writing (summer 2011), this step has not been taken.

Indirect discrimination – imposing conditions on everyone that effectively mean that individuals are favoured, or put at a disadvantage, because of their group identity. It is not regarded as an excuse that practices have a long history or are neutral policies not intended as discriminatory. Settings, services and organisations are responsible for actively exploring the impact of any policy or rules. Such behaviour can be unlawful, unless differential treatment can be shown to be a justifiable method to meet a legitimate aim.

Positive discrimination: generally it is not lawful to treat somebody with a protected characteristic more favourably than, say, colleagues, other parents or peers. The argument might be that this action was to counteract previous disadvantage. The boundaries between affirmative action, or reasonable adjustments, and positive discrimination can be uncertain. Any doubts should be reconciled by legal advice.

Victimisation – treating people, or those close to them (such as children), in a negative way as a consequence of their challenge to discriminatory treatment on the basis of their protected characteristic/group identity.

Segregation – separating a person from others, or making distinctions in a service that effectively separate on the basis of group identity, and with no justifiable reason that would be beneficial to that person.

Scope for exceptions

Equality legislation for race, religion or faith and sex across the UK applies to all races and faiths, both sexes and any sexual orientation. Sex discrimination legislation was originally introduced in response to discrimination against women. However, from the outset, protection in law applied equally to men. So early years provision could not decide to turn away male applicants for posts or to provide men with a different job description on the sole basis of their sex. The same principle applies for legislation relevant to race, religion or faith.

In terms of recruitment or allocation of responsibility within an established team, it is unlawful to treat people differently only on the grounds of their sex, race or faith. Exceptions can be made only if the sex of a member of staff, or a skill perhaps like fluency in languages, can be justified as a proportionate means to reach a legitimate end. This concept is similar to the previous term - a genuine occupational qualification (GOQ).

Managers and any employers are definitely advised to check that their GOQ approach under previous legislation complies fully with the new provisions. The process of identifying exceptions never applies to direct discrimination of any kind, or to claims of victimisation or harassment. You also need proper legal advice to clarify what you can and cannot ask applicants within the recruitment and interviewing process. Broadly you are able to ask questions that will enable you to make reasonable adjustments to employ this applicant.

Figure 2.2 UK society has changed; young children and their interests are much the same

UN Convention

The UN Convention on the Rights of the Child 1989 was the first international agreement in which the rights of children worldwide were detailed in one document. The UK signed the Convention in 1991. Consequently, central government has to ensure that the laws and practice regarding children meet the standards established in the Convention. A rights, and responsibilities, approach has steadily informed some new law and guidance. Within the UK, Scotland was the leading nation in ensuring that the UN Convention on the Rights of the Child was integrated into new legislation. The outstanding exception for UK law as regards the Convention remains the refusal to bring children under the same legal protection as adults against common assault.

The UN Convention is organised by a series of articles, describing the rights of children and young people up to the age of 18 years. Some relevant statements include the following:

Article 2: the right of non-discrimination and that all the rights within the Convention apply to all children equally, whatever their race, sex, religion, language, disability, opinion or family background.

Article 14: parents have a duty to provide children with guidance. However, children have the right to choose their own religion and to express their own views as soon as they are able to decide for themselves.

Article 20: when children cannot be cared for within their own family, the children's race, religion, culture and language must all be taken into consideration in decisions about an alternative home.

Article 30: Children of minority communities and indigenous populations have the right to enjoy their own culture and to practise their own religion and language.

If you want to find out more

- Children's Law Centre – the law in Northern Ireland, **www.childrenslawcentre.org** (accessed 27 July 2011).
- Children's Legal Centre – law in England and Wales, **www.childrenslegalcentre.com** (accessed 27 July 2011).
- Equality and Human Rights Commission, **www.equalityhumanrights.com** (accessed 27 July 2011).
- Equality Commission for Northern Ireland, **www.equalityni.org** (accessed 27 July 2011).
- Scottish Child Law Centre – the law in Scotland, **www.sclc.org.uk** (accessed 27 July 2011).
- UNICEF has a section for the UN Convention on the Rights of the Child, **www.unicef.org/rightsite/index.html** (accessed 27 July 2011).

Policy for equality

The early years of the 21st century have seen a significant shift towards equality as an active approach and integral to all aspects of practice. Equality regarding any group identity cannot be treated as an afterthought or optional add-on activity. Effective equality practice does not stop with addressing negative views or removing inappropriate resources. Professional practice has to be that you actively promote a positive outlook and are ready to deal with possible blocks to inclusion before a situation becomes anywhere close to unacceptable professional practice.

Guidance relevant to early learning

Every setting needs a clear policy on equality issues as they affect everyday practice. In many cases such a policy is a legal requirement; otherwise a clear policy is an integral part of good and effective equality practice. Each nation in the UK has an early years framework. Equality issues are raised in each guidance document about supporting the learning of young children. The exact wording differs, but guidance documents generally commit to ensuring equality of opportunity on the basis of gender, disability, ethnic group, faith and cultural background. Descriptive examples of experiences and resources promote the twin aims of enabling young children to feel positive about their sources of identity and steadily to extend their understanding of family backgrounds and perspectives that are less familiar.

If you want to find out more

- England: the *Early Years Foundation Stage,* the birth-to-five framework, is under revision at the time of writing (summer 2011). Proposals online at **www.education. gov.uk/consultations/index.cfm?action=consultationDetails&consultationId=1747 &external=no&menu=1**
- Northern Ireland: CCEA (2011) *Curricular Guidance for Pre-school Education,* **www.rewardinglearning.org.uk/curriculum/pre_school/index.asp** and CCEA (2006) **Understanding the Foundation Stage, www.nicurriculum.org.uk/docs/foundation_ stage/UF_web.pdf**
- Scotland: Learning and Teaching Scotland (2010) *Pre-birth to Three: Positive Outcomes for Scotland's Children and Families,* **www.ltscotland.org.uk/ earlyyears/** and The Scottish Government (2008) *Curriculum for Excellence: Building the Curriculum 3 – A Framework for Learning and Teaching,* **www. ltscotland.org.uk/buildingyourcurriculum/policycontext/btc/btc3.asp**
- Wales: Welsh Assembly (2008) *Framework for Children's Learning for 3 to 7-year-olds in Wales,* **http://wales.gov.uk/topics/educationandskills/schoolshome/ curriculuminwales/arevisedcurriculumforwales/foundationphase/?lang=en** Also a *Birth to Three Framework* for Wales is in process at the time of writing.

Written policy

You need to check for any local requirements, but it probably works best now to develop a general policy that clearly applies to all equality applications. There could be a great deal of repetition if you try to draft separate policies for ethnic group and culture, faith, language, gender and disability. The Equality Act 2010 for England, Wales and Scotland clearly encourages a more holistic approach, while having due regard to the distinct issues.

The Pre-School Learning Alliance recommends writing a Single Equality Scheme and offers some key ideas (**www.pre-school.org.uk/practitioners/inclusion/461/single-equality-scheme**). Early Years Equality also offers an *Early Years Single Equality Strategy* written by Chrissy Meleady (2011).

Neither group provision nor childminders should try to draft policies starting from a blank sheet of paper. This section offers general points, but you are strongly advised to use available resources from:

- advisors in your local area appropriate to your part of the early years, school and out-of-school services
- supportive materials from your local authority
- your coordinator for the local childminding network
- national professional organisations relevant to your part of services for children and families (see below).

If you want to find out more

The following professional organisations offer information and specific publications relevant to understanding the law and developing an equality policy.

- Early Years – the organisation for young children in Northern Ireland, **www.early-years.org/**
- National Childminding Association, **www.ncma.org.uk**
- National Day Nurseries Association, **www.ndna.org.uk**
- Northern Ireland Childminding Association, **www.nicma.org/cms/index.php**
- Pre-School Learning Alliance, **www.pre-school.org.uk**
- Scottish Childminding Association, **www.childminding.org/**

Policy into practice

Early years provision is required to have a named practitioner who will support the team on practice issues related to disability. Known as the special educational needs coordinator (SENCO), this role has sometimes evolved to become a more general equality coordinator. The person who takes this kind of special responsibility offers a lead, should be ready to promote discussion and actively support continued professional development in the team. This practitioner does not take all responsibility for equality practice in a setting – any more than child protection is handed over totally to the designated person for safeguarding, or the person for support on guiding children's behaviour. Equality, like these other important practice issues, is a matter of shared professional responsibility.

Any policy needs to be open to discussion and review, and an exchange of opinions within a team can raise important practical issues, as well as air misunderstandings or disagreements (see the examples in Chapter 9). Any policy attains real meaning only when it is put into practice day by day and an equality perspective affects all your work. Practitioners in the childminding service also need to have equivalent policies, probably briefer than for group provision, which are still a public statement about your service.

A written policy works as a clear statement of the commitment of the setting, or your personal commitment, to equality and, in brief, how such a commitment affects all aspects of your practice. Think about your choice of words. For instance, I think it is advisable to use phrases like 'active recognition of' different identities, rather than a phrase like 'regardless of ...'. The second choice of words can, unfortunately, suggest that you overlook family or other identity. You might consider a key opening paragraph that focuses on children, perhaps to highlight that you aim to create a harmonious atmosphere in which individual differences are seen as assets. You want all children to feel proud of what contributes to their personal identity.

Different elements make up the whole framework for an early years, school or out-of-school service and would include that you will behave so as to achieve key elements of equality practice. You will do the following:

- Organise every aspect of the service with careful attention to equality. A clear focus on equality includes where and how you promote the service. In group settings, equality affects your admissions system, staff recruitment, selection and training within a team.
- Ensure that all children are welcome and fully included in the regular routines and experiences of your service. Part of this commitment has to be about resolving any issues that prevent children being included.
- Offer personal care that meets the individual needs of children, always with emotional warmth, and that is attentive to their dignity and responsive to family preferences.
- Ensure that any individual care or learning needs will be met in ways that enable children to feel full members of your setting or service.
- Meet children's spiritual needs in ways that are respectful to everyone. Meeting those needs will not entail separate experiences unless this option is appropriate (for instance, a private room for prayer).
- Respect different ways of learning and ensure that individual children can access the resources and experiences on offer.
- Promote respect and courtesy between children through a positive approach to guiding behaviour, which is appropriate to their age and understanding. You will deal with unacceptable words, actions or attempted ill treatment.
- Create an accessible and balanced learning environment, with experiences and resources that actively show respect for all children and support an extension of their understanding beyond what is currently familiar.

- Work in an open and courteous partnership with each parent or family carer, being willing to describe what you do and why, dealing respectfully with any differences of opinion or belief and explaining if it is not possible to meet a family's preference.

Policy and strategy

Any policy has to work alongside reflective and good practice. No written policy will do the work alone; it has to be put into practice through the words and actions of practitioners. A policy is a statement of intentions for your practice or service. So policies lay out key principles and values that inform and guide your work. A strategy explains how good intentions will be put into practice, the details of procedures or the choices to be made under given circumstances. The strategy might also be called an implementation programme.

> ### What does it mean?
>
> **Policy:** key intentions, values or principles that guide a given area of practice.
>
> **Strategy:** procedures, steps or preferred approaches for dealing with situations arising that are relevant to this policy.

A broad strategy could be about exact steps to be followed, for instance if a team member persisted in biased communication practice that resulted in some families receiving considerably more attention than others. However, strategy that is understood and discussed could be more about the balance of what is done. An example would be that children who use offensive language are told firmly that the words are unacceptable and why. However, practitioners are still responsive in helping with any conflict that provoked the words.

A realistic view of policy that brings in strategy is not restricted to equality. For instance, your policy about health and safety will not itself keep children or adults safe – no matter how beautifully drafted or laminated. An acceptable level of health and safety is delivered by people who follow what has been agreed and are ready to ask questions for any situation that is unclear. Policy on equality and any related areas of practice has to come alive day by day. A good standard of professionalism is that practitioners raise promptly any dilemmas they face, or when one policy in practice appears to go counter to the requirements of another policy.

No policy will cover every conceivable situation in detail and it would be unwise to try.
- Focus on the positives in the wording of any policy – what will you offer and promote? Much like an effective policy on behaviour, you do not want an equality policy that is imbalanced towards listing all the situations you will not tolerate in the name of good practice.

- Your policy needs to state your commitment to clear communication with parents and other family carers, your willingness to listen and seek to understand what matters to each and every family. But avoid any wording that suggests partnership will always mean following parents' requests. Agreement will not always be possible and practitioners need to feel confident to give themselves time to think, or consult in a team situation.
- Equality policy, linked with behaviour, may say that offensive badges, T-shirts or written material are not welcome within a school or after-school club. However, local conditions will determine the detail of decisions that need to be discussed.
- An inclusive approach to the physical care needs of children can raise issues around existing policies – for example, about what medication practitioners can give to children or whether three-year-olds are expected to be reliably toilet trained. You need a general statement of commitment and should be swift to review policy assumptions that could act so as to exclude a child.

Reflection and review

Part of policy and strategy has to be a shared understanding of how you recognise successful outcomes from the policy. Of course, success is not a one-off, or final 'We've done it!' Nor will it be effective practice for children if their important adults are weighed down by obligation to track and prove particular outcomes. However, all individuals or teams need to explore what you will be pleased to see and hear in your time with children and families. You might consider the following questions:

- What current examples of practice, involving actual children and families, are able to show that your policy is working in an active way?
- Are the details of the policy clear to you and to everyone in the team? In what ways have questions or comments highlighted different interpretations of policy in daily practice?
- Are the details of the policy clear to the families who use your service? If conversation within partnership raises issues, is there good reason to revisit the policy?
- Are your policy and practice over equality clear to other local professionals with whom you work?
- In what ways do you use the opportunities of continued professional development, part of which can be from training?
- What are your information systems for ensuring that you are up to date with any changes in local or national guidance or how the law could affect you? You cannot assume that someone else will always tell you face to face.

One way of evaluating equality practice can be to monitor and collect numerical data. Services, including early years and schools, are expected to collect data about the group background of children and families, and in more general the users of their services and any facilities. The aim of collecting such statistics is to establish a reliable baseline from which to launch improvements and changes to services where any groups appear to be excluded. Parents should have easy access to the data of their children and will provide the group identity choices for children, such as ethnic group or faith.

Pause for reflection

The written material of any setting has to be reasonably concise. It is expensive in time and money to produce many long documents, and few parents will get round to reading pages and pages of details. So it is almost inevitable that you will have brief phrases that sum up your approach. You need to be able to explain – to people who are not fellow professionals in your field – what the words mean in practice day by day in the setting.

Look at the following examples. What else would you need to say, perhaps to a parent, to bring these phrases alive? Ideally, think of a good example within your own practice of 'What I do'. If these are phrases in a written policy, are there better ways to express that aim?

'We celebrate diversity in the nursery.'

'Here we work to empower disabled children.'

'I show respect for every child's home language.'

'We take a multicultural approach to caring.'

'All nurseries in our company are committed to gender equality.'

'We treat children differently in order to treat them equally.'

'My aim is to treat all children with equal concern.'

'We offer an anti-bias early years curriculum.'

'I encourage all the children to respect faiths other than their own.'

'We want to ensure that all children feel included.'

Chapter

3

Active support for both sexes

All societies take a stance on how to raise girls and boys and how to ensure that they grow into the women and men wanted by this social or cultural group. UK society is no exception to this general rule and, for many decades, the pattern was one in which men and boys were more highly valued than women and girls.

Equality over sex has entered a more even-handed phase and concerns are now properly expressed about the experiences of boys and whether circumstances combine to disrupt their learning and well being. Sex equality law and guidance never deny that there are differences between the sexes. The equality obligation is about ensuring that differences are not treated as if they are deficiencies.

The main sections of this chapter cover:
- difference, inequality, equal chances
- focus on childhood
- reflection on gender equality.

Difference, inequality, equal chances

As with other equality areas, the key issues around gender do not make much sense without some social history.

During the first half of the 20th century, laws and entrenched social attitudes in the UK encouraged a view that women were less able, less responsible and less important in society than men. The decades from the end of the 19th century and into the first part of the 20th saw some improvement from a situation in which women had scarcely higher legal status than children. Some basic rights, including being able to vote, were finally granted to the female half of the adult population. However, many legal and social inequalities continued into the second half of the century.

Social attitudes

For many generations, the avowed theory was that women would care for their families and raise children. This role was allegedly respected, but over decades most messages to women and girls told them loudly that the male, breadwinner role was much more valuable. This outlook conveniently overlooked the fact that many working-class women had held down paid work over the decades when middle-class women had been forced to resign from professions as soon as they were married.

Some of these social attitudes persist, although not always in the same format. In the 21st century, women who choose to put their energies into raising their children are still vulnerable to criticism, sometimes from fellow females. Many more fathers are now the main carer at home, at least for a while. They, too, experience, although in a different way, the social value that work really has to be paid in order to deserve respect. We still have some distance to go before the vital role of caring for children is genuinely valued for either sex in our society.

Over much of the 20th century, it was common to hear that women should not be in positions of responsibility because they were too emotional – meant as a criticism. Yet aggressive behaviour in boys or men was not treated as a dubious emotional reaction. The behaviour was more likely to be interpreted as 'decisive', evidence of the ability to manage and lead others. Female leaders, meanwhile, risked being labelled as 'bossy' or 'shrill'. That possibility still exists in the early 21st century.

Research and theory

During the 20th century, broad social attitudes about men and women were reflected in the social sciences, despite their claim to be objective. Many prominent names from early psychology and sociology were men. Theories about personality development, moral reasoning and behaviour patterns such as aggression frequently took observations of men or boys as the norm. When a theory did not easily apply to female development or behaviour, then the reaction was rarely to change the theory. The explanation was far more often that the female pattern was a deviation from 'normal' development or a sign of problems.

During the 1970s there was a strong reaction against this bias within the social sciences. Many female psychologists and sociologists worked to value the different female patterns and to build theory and research that were a genuine reflection of both sexes. Feminist approaches are now well established and in some ways have evened up the discussion. However, feminism has subdivided into many strands, some of which are in serious dispute with each other. The female sex has the capacity to be as dogmatic as the male. Feminist perspectives have a great deal to offer the debate over sex and gender. However, it is crucial to recall that opinions should be clearly distinguished from evidence – either research or more informal observations – and that both are open to considered challenge (Archer, 2004).

In a fair society it should be possible to ask, 'Why does it matter?' if females and males are different in other than the obvious physical attributes. Surely any society benefits from diversity? However, it is still sometimes difficult to discuss female–male differences in a calm way.

Part of the problem is historical, because over decades any apparent differences between females and males were interpreted as evidence of female inferiority. There are positive signs of change: that all parts of society, not least children, need a blend of perspectives and abilities, some of which may be more on the masculine side and some on the feminine. Different should not necessarily mean better or worse, superior or inferior.

Simon Baron-Cohen (2003) describes his extreme wariness about going into print with his research about male and female brain functioning. He presents findings that the male and female brains, on average, seem to work differently. Intriguingly, Baron-Cohen's starting point was that the male brain seems to be more prone to patterns that can create extremes: the type of obsessiveness that may be labelled as genius or within the autistic spectrum, depending on the focus of concentrated activity.

Despite his careful explanation, Baron-Cohen's work has sometimes been misinterpreted: that the stronger male tendency to systemise and analyse must mean that men have a higher IQ. The stronger female tendency to empathise is an average difference, not a statement about overall intelligence in either direction. It has to be said also that some fellow scientists disagree with Baron-Cohen's interpretation of the data (Eliot, 2009).

Different – so what?

In one important way girls and boys are very different from each other. The sex of children is a biological distinction, which is defined by chromosomes and

Figure 3.1 Young boys and girls enjoy physically lively games

EQUALITY AND INCLUSION IN EARLY CHILDHOOD

anatomical differences. The significant pattern of physical changes brought about by hormonal changes over puberty means that girls grow up into young women and boys grow into young men. A very small minority of children are born with indeterminate sex, because they have a combination of male and female physical attributes. Some children and young people come to question their sexual identity and may seek to change sex (transgender). But most children will start and remain the same sex, and they all need a positive outlook on the adults they will eventually become.

Gender is a social concept or construct: the total of all the attributes typically associated with a given sex. A child's or adult's behaviour is the observable version of how inclinations and beliefs emerge to be visible through actions. Behavioural traits stretch over a broad continuum of masculinity and femininity and there is noticeable within-sex variation. The values and social mores of some cultural and social groups operate so as to restrict this possible variation and keep either sex within the confines of what is judged to be the right behaviour. Anxiety to fit in means that older children and adolescents sometimes 'police' themselves (Frosh et al., 2003).

There are several related questions about the personal and social development of the two sexes, and these issues are often muddled in conversation or argument. The first two broad questions are about research evidence.

1 Are men and women, boys and girls, consistently different from each other? If so, then in what way(s)? Also, are any differences statistically significant and found reliably in more than one or two studies?

2 If there are predictable sex differences, then to what extent is this situation best explained by biology and the genetic pattern? To what extent can we determine that the impact of personal experiences starts in very early childhood?

This second question is rarely, if ever, expressed now as a blunt nature or nurture. The majority of discussion is about a blend. The arguments are about how much can be attributed to biology and this debate has accentuated with disputes over what research into the human brain does, or does not, show about sex differences. In this chapter I have aimed to negotiate these troubled waters, to enable readers to understand the main themes for practice.

The second set of questions homes in on the social relevance of any differences. Regardless of the details of any reliable data:

1 In what ways does it matter if there are observable sex differences in behaviour, skills, brain functioning and other aspects?

2 Is there a problem about difference and why? Or could average differences have positive implications for appropriately different ways of how adults should support girls and boys?

were given messages that would restrict their options and development. Any movement that is genuinely concerned with best practice must be ready to reflect, and that is what has happened over gender equality. There has been an increasing awareness of the messages being given to boys and the responsibility to address their well being and development.

Fairness and equal chances

A fair and even-handed approach is to show equal levels of nurture, respect and concern for all children. Girls and boys deserve active support, so they can feel positive about their personal identity by gender. Neither sex should be weighed in the balance and found wanting, because their interests or behaviour do not fit an adult-imposed pattern.

On gender, as on race, I think it is unacceptable for adults – practitioners, academics, parents or anyone – to blame children for past or present inequalities within the adult world. Young boys and girls cannot be held responsible for the power relations that were established before they were born. I believe it is very clear in this section, as with race (page 17), that I do support addressing children's behaviour – actions and words – to counteract any negative outlooks that children are already learning.

The early years professional world is overwhelmingly female. This sex imbalance is not the result of some plot by women, so recognition of this fact implies no criticism whatsoever. The main reasons for such a female profession include social views that still judge working with young children as more 'women's work'. Contact with younger children is often seen as less valuable than teaching late primary or secondary pupils, with the consequent lower status, pay and conditions of many of the jobs. However, the end result is that unreflective female teams can slip into judging boys against their own childhood memories and current worries about liveliness or ensuring children cooperate in very adult-led activities.

Children will not be supported in developing a strong sense of personal identity if practitioners believe equality practice means overlooking differences. Good practice over ethnic group or cultural identity has challenged the cliché of 'I treat them all the same.' There was a time lag in challenging that kind of unreflective thinking as applied to gender equality. For a while, early years practitioners were directed by some childcare courses and textbooks to ignore the differences between boys and girls and focus on the similarities.

Such advice made no more sense for adult behaviour towards girls and boys than it did for an approach to children over ethnic group flagged up by skin colour. The end result of that kind of 'treating them all the same' was that, for too long, White practitioners treated Black children as if they were White, or interpreted those children's needs as special needs: a variation from the White norm. There is a real risk that female practitioners, claiming not to make any distinction, may treat boys as children who fail to fit the 'girl' pattern. Boys deserve to be treated respectfully as young males. They should not be repackaged as noisy little girls who stand up to pee.

Of course, female childhoods vary. Some, like my own, were dominated by digging holes, climbing trees, building dens and go-karts, as well as taking immense pleasure in dolls, books, cooking and dressing-up. Towards the end of the 20th century, more active and outdoor pursuits have staged a successful comeback against pressures to get many young children to sit quietly, 'do their learning' indoors and tolerate a great deal of adult direction of their play.

In the name of early education, there has been a great deal of discussion within early years of 'play with a purpose' and 'well-structured play'. The purposes and structure became, in too many instances, those of adults, not envisaged and chosen by children themselves (Lindon, 2010). The end result of over-direction by adults was negative for many children, especially when it went alongside a very cautious approach to risk and adventurous activity (Lindon, 2011). The combination of over-direction and anxiety had the greatest adverse impact on the more lively, physically enthusiastic, outdoor-loving children, and many (not all) of these have been boys.

Figure 3.2 Boys often flourish with generous time outdoors – but so do girls

Awareness of your own behaviour

You and your colleagues, as well as the parents with whom you have contact, have all been influenced during childhood. There is no need to feel personally at fault about assumptions and expectations learned in your childhood. However, you are responsible now for thinking about your views, being willing to question some of

- Look at how the toys are organised into different sections. What is the basis for this organisation?
- Look at the packaging of toys and play materials. If children are shown on the boxes, are they boys, girls or both? What are they doing?
- If you were a child, might you conclude that some toys and kinds of equipment were more for the opposite sex?
- Are there different versions of the same item of equipment? For instance, are bikes or scooters offered in different colours or styles for girls and boys?
- Are there some sections that seem genuinely for both sexes? What are they?

If possible, take a child who is five years or older with you on this trip (your own child or a niece or nephew, perhaps). Ask children for their opinion, including which toys are supposed to be for boys or girls.

If you want to find out more

- Archer, J. (2004) 'The trouble with "Doing Boy"'. *The Psychologist,* 17, 3, 132–9, **www.thepsychologist.org.uk/archive/archive_home.cfm?volumeID=17&editionID=104&ArticleID=673**
- Baron-Cohen, S. (2003) *The Essential Difference: Men, Women and the Extreme Male Brain.* London: Allen Lane.
- Bilton, H., with Brent Early Years Team (2005) *Learning Outdoors: Improving the Quality of Young Children's Play Outdoors.* London: David Fulton Publishers.
- Browne, N. (2004) *Gender Equity in the Early Years.* Maidenhead: Open University Press.
- Department for Education and Skills (2007) *Gender and Education: the Evidence on Pupils in England.*London: DfES, **www.education.gov.uk/publications/standard/publicationDetail/Page1/DFES-00389-2007**
- Eliot, L. (2009) *Pink Brain Blue Brain – How Small Differences Grow into Troublesome Gaps and What We Can Do about It.* New York: Houghton Mifflin Harcourt. Listen to Lise Eliot online (accessed 1 September 2011), **http://fora.tv/2009/09/29/Lise_Eliot_Pink_Brain_Blue_Brain**
- Featherstone, S. and Bayley, R. (2005) *Boys and Girls Come Out to Play: Not Better Or Worse, Just Different.* Husbands Bosworth. Featherstone Education.
- Frosh, S., Phoenix, A. and Pattman, R. (2003) 'The trouble with boys', *The Psychologist,* 16, 2, 84–7, **www.thepsychologist.org.uk/archive/archive_home.cfm?volumeID=16&editionID=91&ArticleID=521**
- Healy, J. (2004) *Your Child's Growing Mind: A Practical Guide to Brain Development and Learning from Birth to Adolescence.* New York: Broadway.
- Holland, P. (2003) *We Don't Play With Guns Here: War, Weapon and Superhero Play in the Early Years.* Maidenhead: Open University Press.
- Kahn, T. (2011) *The XY Factor: Addressing Gender in the Early Years.* London: Pre-School Learning Alliance.
- Lindon, J. (2001) *Understanding Children's Play.* Cheltenham: Nelson Thornes.

- Lindon, J. (2010) *Child-initiated Play: Positive Relationships in the Early Years.* London: Practical Pre-School Books.
- Lindon, J. (2011) *Too Safe for Their Good? Helping Children Learn about Risk and Lifeskills.* London: National Children's Bureau.
- Lindon, J. and Lindon, L. (2012) *Leadership and Early Years Professionalism.* London: Hodder Education. (Chapter 1 in particular.)
- Maccoby, E.E. (1998) *The Two Sexes: Growing UApart, Coming Together.* Cambridge, MA: Harvard University Press.
- Ofsted (2008) *White Boys from Low-Income Backgrounds,* **www.ofsted.gov.uk/resources/white-boys-low-income-backgrounds-good-practice-schools**
- Skelton, C. and Hall, E. (2001) *The Development of Gender Roles in Young Children: A Review of Policy and the Literature.* Manchester: Equal Opportunities Commission.
- Yelland, N. (ed) (1998) *Gender in Early Childhood.* London: Routledge.

colonised countries had a real culture. The slave trade, although not justified completely, was still sometimes presented as an unfortunate economic necessity.

Generations of children grew up with a conviction that the White British way of life was not only the best but had brought light into the darkness (a very common image) of 'primitive' countries. A liberal outlook was that people from the African or Indian continent and the Caribbean could be educated and therefore become 'more like us'. This outlook, if expressed still by the eldest generation, sounds desperately patronising. However, it should be distinguished, historically, from the overtly racist outlook of that time: that 'non-White' people would always be inferior and were unwelcome as residents in the UK.

The legacy of history meant that Black residents of the UK frequently met prejudiced attitudes and active discrimination. By the 1970s and onwards, enough people (White as well as Black) felt strongly that the situation was completely unacceptable and that positive action had to be taken, through legislation and direct challenge to people's attitudes in action.

Attitudes in practice

Racist attitudes entered the way that organisations and administration worked on a daily basis. Systems and procedures have to be developed originally by individuals. Those people may have been explicitly racist, but were just as likely to have made decisions on the basis of assumptions that they simply never questioned. Once discriminatory systems are in place, they give support to individuals who are openly racist. The sense of 'but this is how we do it' encourages a sense of inertia for those who are much less racist in outlook or intention. It is hard work to challenge a set of procedures that carries the weight of tradition and is presented as normal. There are strong parallels with how some assumptions about gender and disability became deeply rooted in administrative or employment practices, creating institutional blocks to equality.

Take another **perspective**

For understandable historical reasons, a considerable amount of emphasis in racial equality has been on racist attitudes held by White people about Black ethnic groups. Some sources of racial bigotry continue in that blunt vein.

However, equality practice within a highly diverse society, as is now the case with the UK, has to be even-handed. Best practice for equality has to recognise that members of ethnic groups, who experience discrimination, can themselves be bigoted and rejecting about other groups. The Runnymede Trust (**www.runnymedetrust.org**), for instance, has material about the need to challenge homophobia within some Black subcultures.

Such an outlook will sit uncomfortably with a simplistic race equality perspective. But a more honest approach about human behaviour is necessary, especially when the aim is to promote positive attitudes and behaviour from early childhood.

There is no secure scientific basis for the concept of race. Attempts to find clear-cut genetic distinctions have consistently shown a high level of variation within any of the groupings that have been tried. Generally speaking, the term 'race' is now used to mean a distinction between groups on the basis of skin colour, ethnic or national origins. Racial bigotry has not been restricted to differences based on skin colour. Anti-Semitism has a long and shameful history in the UK, as well as in other European countries.

Non-English ethnic groups in Britain, such as the Welsh or Scots, can also look back on a history of oppression of their culture and language. It is very usual now, for instance, to hear a wide range of accents on the television or radio. But the eldest generation in the UK often unlearned their Irish, Cornish or other so-called 'regional' accents to increase acceptance in professional occupations and avoid offensive remarks presented as jokes.

Language and culture

Cultural traditions are passed on within families and communities partly through a shared language. Linguistic tradition is therefore part of cultural and ethnic group identity. Respect for family language(s) and accent has to be an integral part of any approach to equality.

Around the world, bilingualism is common and many children grow up learning two or more languages. In countries on mainland Europe, confident use of two languages is normal for many people. However, it is often overlooked that there is a long history in the UK of bilingualism for speakers who have combined knowledge of English with fluency in Welsh, Scottish Gaelic (pronounced 'gallic') and Irish Gaelic. Cornish and Manx (on the Isle of Man) went into decline as daily spoken languages, although both have an active heritage movement.

Yet, until the final decades of the 20th century, the common view in England was that the only 'normal' language development was for children to learn English and then to study one or more 'foreign' languages at secondary school. The language movements in Wales and Scotland struggled against active attempts to suppress daily use of languages other than English. For instance, within the first half of the 20th century some teachers in Wales felt justified in a policy of caning children for speaking Welsh in ordinary conversation.

It was therefore not surprising that many professionals took a negative approach to families from minority ethnic groups who became resident through immigration from the 1960s and whose first language was not English. Bilingualism was treated as a problem by service providers who were blinkered by their own monolingual situation. Parents were told that they must speak only English to their children, otherwise the children's language development would be disrupted. A fluent home language was often ignored and children's emerging English was treated as their only language, leading to assessment of speaking children as having 'poor' or 'no' language. School pupils could end up in remedial classes for no reason other than lack of fluent English.

Over the second half of the 20th century, there was a slow but significant change in official treatment of languages other than English. Active bilingual movements took root in Wales, Scotland and Ireland. Welsh, in particular, is the success story of Europe's regional languages. From a precarious existence in mid-Wales, the language is now prominent in the early years and school curriculum, and established in all aspects of public life.

Early years practice, as for schools, is appropriately expected now to respect children and families who speak more than one language and to show active respect for the home language(s). Reflective practitioners still need to remain alert about assumptions. I still occasionally hear children described as 'not talking much', when the problem is more accurately that the practitioner cannot understand what children are saying in their home language.

Some children are age-appropriate fluent in a language which few, or maybe no, practitioners are able to speak. Children also need a shared vocabulary for play with their peers. They are very adept at finding ways around a lack of shared fluent language, but the play of over-threes becomes ever more integrated with spoken language. The important issue for best practice, starting in early childhood, is to combine active respect for family languages alongside the appropriate focus on helping all children to become fluent in the shared, national language, which is English. A strong focus on language development, talking, listening and building a large spoken vocabulary is equally important for monolingual White children from highly disadvantaged backgrounds.

Families with a travelling lifestyle

The history of travelling families within Europe goes back many centuries, and the travelling lifestyle has more than one origin.

The word 'gypsy' comes from Egypt, where many of the itinerant Romani (Romany or Roma) people had lived before travelling into Europe. It seems likely that Romani Gypsies came to Egypt originally from India. This travelling community has been present in the UK for about five centuries.

As mentioned on page 9, at one time equality advisors were firm that the word 'gypsy' should not be used, since it was an offensive term. The Romani Gypsies definitely wish to be known by this term and one motive is to distinguish their origins from the Irish travelling community, who have been in England for about 150 years. The third broad group is the newer arrivals such as new age travellers. Some of this latter group took to the road over the 1960s–70s, but some Londoners who fled the bombing during the Second World War had already become permanent travellers. The terms Traveller, Irish Traveller or Romani Gypsy tend to be given capital letters in order to indicate that the terms cover a distinct ethnic group identity.

Gypsies and Irish Travellers have been fully recognised as ethnic groups because they have a shared culture, language and beliefs. They are therefore covered legally against discrimination. The cultural code of many Romani communities is guided by romaniya (Gypsy laws) customs and rules that distinguish behaviour that is *vujo* (pure) and that which is *marime* (polluted). Gypsies speak Romani, a language close to Hindi. Irish Travellers have a distinct language, known as Shelta, Gammon or Cant, which is different from Gaelic.

Travellers from any of the nomadic groups frequently experience hostility from the settled population. Poor relations are often provoked by lack of proper sites on which travelling families can stop. The situation was aggravated by the removal in 1994 of a legal duty on local authorities to provide sites. Some long-standing travelling groups themselves harbour deep suspicions about the settled population, whom they call *gaujos* or *gorgios*. This wariness is sometimes fuelled by specific ill treatment of their children in schools or fears about the dangers to the children outside the immediate protection of their family.

Early years or school staff have sometimes been less than enthusiastic about children from travelling families because of the conviction that the families will soon move on: 'So what's the point?' This outlook is unacceptable. Families sometimes stay in one location for some or most of a calendar year. Some family movements follow a planned circuit involved in running a travelling circus or fairground, taking seasonal work on a circuit of farms or moving by canal barge. You would not avoid making an effort for a child whose parents' professional commitments might move them on in the near future, so there is no justification for being less than fully attentive to Gypsy and Traveller children.

Even if families do move on, a positive experience for child and parent in your setting will support the whole family when they make a relationship with the next early years centre or school. Many local authorities now have support services for Gypsy and Traveller families, either as a dedicated team or as part of services for families from a range of minority ethnic groups.

> **If you want to find out more**

- Belton, B. (2005) *Questioning Gypsy Identity: Ethnic Narratives in Britain and America*. Walnut Creek, CA: AltaMira Press.
- The Travellers' School Charity, **www.travellersschool.org.uk**
- Traveller Law Research Unit, **www.law.cf.ac.uk/tlru**
- Trentham Books has several titles – check the website to see which may be most relevant to your work, **www.trentham-books.co.uk**

Use a search engine like Google for 'Traveller Education Service' and you bring up many local services around the UK. Some have developed books, photo resources and posters that they are happy to share or sell.

Refugee families and asylum seekers

The word 'refugee' has a specific legal meaning under the 1951 UN Convention Relating to the Status of Refugees. Refugees are people who have left their own country and are unable to return 'owing to a well-founded fear of being persecuted for reasons of race, religion, nationality, membership of a particular social group or political opinion'. In order to stay in the UK, individuals or families who arrive as asylum seekers have to apply for official refugee status. Children and young people under the age of 18 years, who arrive unaccompanied by a parent or other adult carer, automatically become the responsibility of the local authority.

What does it mean?

Refugees: people who have left their own country through fear of persecution or the danger of remaining in their home. They have crossed international borders in search of safety.

Asylum seekers: people who have left their country of origin and applied for asylum in the UK. They are waiting to know whether they will be given refugee status and be permitted to stay.

In addition to becoming accustomed to a new country, some families have left their homes under distressing circumstances and perhaps with very little chance to prepare their children. Adults and children may have traumatic memories of the disruptions that turned them into refugees. Even very young children may have seen terrible sights and know that members of their family, immediate or more extended, are still living or fighting in dangerous areas. The refugee families may be living in temporary accommodation with uncertainty about where they will live in the near future and whether the family will be allowed to stay in the UK.

The Immigration and Asylum Act 1999 led to increased dispersal of refugee and asylum-seeker families away from London and the south-east of England where many had settled after arrival. The aim was to relieve the pressure on a few local authorities which were heavily responsible for the families and saying ever more loudly that the duty of care was a national issue. Whatever the intentions, the resulting relocation was often far from smooth.

Support and understanding will be essential to help both the children and their parents. It is also possible that tensions may develop in the local neighbourhood, from resistance to the families' arrival and possibly fuelled by beliefs that refugee families are getting material advantages not available to existing residents. Sudden relocation of families around the UK has not helped local services to ease their entry. However, some areas, like Glasgow (one of the three UK cities other than London with more than 2,000 school pupils from refugee and asylum-seeker families), have worked hard to support early years and school services. The city has also created facilities, such as play areas, that clearly support the whole local community and offer a chance for adults to come together over the common ground of having children.

If you want to find out more

- Hyder, T. (2004) *War, Conflict and Play: Working with Refugee Children in the Early Years.* Maidenhead: Open University Press.
- Refugee Council (020 7820 3000) **www.refugeecouncil.org.uk** (accessed 27 July 2011).
- Rutter, J. (2003) *Supporting Refugee Children in 21st Century Britain: a Compendium of Essential Information.* Stoke-on-Trent: Trentham Books, **www.trentham-books.co.uk** (accessed 27 July 2011).
- The Children's Legal Centre Home Page for Refugee Children's Rights Project, **www.childrenslegalcentre.com** (accessed 27 July 2011).
- The UN Refugee Agency, **www.unhcr.org.uk/about-us/the-uk-and-asylum.html**

Learning from childhood

Children tend to assume that the family life of other people is much the same as their own, until experience shows them the level of diversity. For anyone, what they know best can seem to be the natural or obvious way of organising a life or raising children. If adults remain with relatively narrow horizons, then different ways may be judged as odd, exotic or suspect. Early years practitioners have a responsibility to address narrow views or rejection of less familiar ways.

Figure 4.1 Young children are interested in physical differences

Cultural traditions affect everyone

Unreflective adults may take the stance that they talk 'normally'; it is other people who have a 'strong accent'. Or people say in a puzzled way, 'I bring up my children the way I was raised; I don't have a cultural tradition.' But experience of culture is not something that just happens to other people – everyone has a cultural background, just as everyone has an ethnic group to which they belong.

Pause for reflection

Please consider your own ethnic group identity and sense of cultural heritage.

How would you describe yourself in words? What are your family origins in terms of ethnic group and/or nationality?

Within your daily life, in what ways do your habits and choices reflect your own cultural background?

If you find it hard to get started, you might think about food and drink, how you dress, what you do in your leisure time or the family celebrations in which you are involved.

Reflect on your childhood, whether it was within your birth family or an alternative form of upbringing. In what ways did you build an understanding of your identity and family allegiances? What made 'you'?

If possible, share some of these ideas and memories with colleagues or fellow students. Take care to show active respect for the reflections and reminiscences of everyone.

Everyone has their own source of ethnicity; all people have their own ethnic origins. So individuals of Celtic origin, Gaelic or Scandinavian are an ethnic group just as much as people of Thai, Moroccan or Bangladeshi origin. Cultural traditions can affect everyday behaviour as well as influence the details of special occasions or festivals. Diet and style of eating, personal hygiene and habits, forms of spoken and non-verbal communication can all be shaped by cultural traditions. Some aspects of culture are rooted in the religious beliefs that have shaped the traditions of a given society or social group. Some patterns of behaviour can therefore persist, even when individuals are not active followers of a particular religious faith. However, 'Muslim' is not a description of ethnic group identity, any more than 'Christian'. When people share a faith that has spread over much of the world, they will often differ in ethnic group, language and cultural tradition.

Pause for reflection

Misuse of the word 'ethnic' can highlight narrow or dismissive views of cultures other than that of the person speaking. In some instances the term is used effectively to mean 'exotic' or non-European.

If tandoori chicken is an example of 'ethnic food', then so is steak and kidney pie. English country dancing is an example of cultural tradition just as much as Greek dances. My most ridiculous example so far was a household catalogue that featured 'ethnic tables' – apparently the words indicated that the style was Indian.

Unfortunate choice of language in some catalogues for play resources perpetuates the idea that there is 'our culture' and there are 'other cultures'. Even companies that offer good-quality resources sometimes have an odd way with words. The words 'multicultural' or 'ethnic' are often used to mean any non-European or 'non-White' source.

- 'Multicultural hats' – what does such a phrase mean exactly? What is the message when the display of hats I saw for sale was all from non-European traditions? The hats did not include flat caps, panama hats or silky headscarves, of the kind worn by the Queen.
- Some companies specify an outfit for a Nigerian child but many propose the cover-all of 'African child'. This huge continent is made up of many countries, cultures, languages, faiths and ways of dressing. General terms such as 'Oriental' or 'Asian' are no more accurate. What assumptions are revealed by this choice of words?
- Whatever your cultural background, try collecting a set of clothes to meet the aim of dressing up as a 'European' child or adult. Is it possible? Does it make any sense at all?

Find some examples of your own and discuss them with colleagues or fellow students.

Adult responsibilities

Young children do not automatically assume that skin colour or other visible group differences mean that people are more or less worthy. However, children who are exposed to bigoted attitudes and actions soon use what they have heard, or the behaviour they have watched. Young children can build a negative image associated with a darker skin colour, or other indicators of ethnic origin, cultural difference or faith.

Prejudice has an impact on how children feel about themselves, as well as their attitude towards others. Those children who are part of the dominant ethnic or cultural group may boost their sense of self-worth by disparaging others. Their pride in their own group, and in themselves as a member of that group, is supported largely by feelings of superiority or by ridiculing others. Negative views learned by some children will gain a stronger hold, like any kind of rejection of other people, if responsible adults do not counteract the dismissive sense of arrogance.

The children who are part of the group to which the prejudice is directed are soon fully aware of this rejection. They are at risk of low self-esteem, or at the very least of downplaying important aspects of their personal and family identity. Young children who are emotionally targeted can develop a very fragile sense of self-worth.

Research in the United States and the UK up to the 1970s established that some Black children, as young as four and five years old, had already encountered sufficiently racist beliefs that they expressed a preference to be White (summary in Milner, 1983). Children's views were usually invited through their reactions to dolls or pictures. Similar research has not continued and both societies have changed, not least with very active movements to support a positive identity for Black children from a diversity of ethnic group backgrounds. There is every reason to suppose that young children still pick up on the attitudes around them and that Black children are still vulnerable, because of crass prejudice linked with skin colour. However, possible reactions could well include the choice to attack verbally in return, rather than assume that bigots are correct.

Practitioners in mainly White areas

Some areas of the UK show very little evidence of ethnic diversity, especially if the focus is on skin colour. The national, cultural and religious origins of local families may have many sources of diversity. However, this fact is not immediately obvious because the majority of the population is White. Some practitioners share the views of other local residents that equality issues around race and cultural tradition are relevant only for urban areas with their 'inner-city race problems'. This mistaken outlook about cities can be as misguided as the naive views held by some urban dwellers about country life. Communities with ethnic group diversity are not all disrupted on a regular basis, although it makes striking newspaper headlines.

In mainly White areas, unreflective practitioners can feel that ethnic group and cultural equality issues are more theoretical than real. The advantages of a mixed local area are undoubtedly that children have first-hand experience of diversity in dress, beliefs, diet and language. The challenge in a non-diverse area is to acknowledge the everyday life of the immediate neighbourhood, which makes sense to young children. Yet practitioners need to extend children's horizons: showing that daily life is different not so very far away, perhaps no more than an hour or so by car or train.

You have a responsibility to show children something of the world beyond their own back door. You also have a responsibility for the future; many children will travel and leave their current local community. The details of equality over ethnic group and cultural tradition should be adjusted to reflect local reality. However, any team or advisory service needs to distinguish between what is appropriate adjustment and what is sneaky avoidance of the issues.

There can be genuine practical problems of finding resources in an area with limited ethnic diversity. Local bookshops or toy suppliers may offer a range that assumes everyone is White or otherwise exotic, temporary visitors. You may need to obtain materials through the many mail-order book or play resources suppliers (see page 175). However, many settings in diverse areas face the same situation. High-street stores do not necessarily reflect the full variety of families living locally.

Scenario

The Whittons Nursery is located in a neighbourhood where there is limited obvious ethnic group diversity; most of the local faces are White. Clare, the manager, wants to use partnership with all parents. She is aware that the previous manager was well intentioned, but made the few parents from non-European backgrounds feel like walking visual aids for special events.

Li-Fong's family are very busy running their restaurant, but had felt under great pressure to be key figures in the nursery's celebration of Chinese New Year. They are relieved that Clare would like to repeat the experience but is ensuring that the event is clearly for everyone, not highly focused on Li-Fong. Clare is also working hard to challenge the belief that has built up in the Whittons team that contact with one family from a particular ethnic group or faith is sufficient to inform everyone about that background or set of beliefs.

With support, the team are now developing a more inclusive outlook on this aspect to their equality practice. For instance, the dolls with Black African features are an integral part of pretend play resources. They are not on display because Rafat has now joined the group.

Once Rafat's family had come to know the team, Clare felt ready to invite suggestions from his mother for stories or music that could complement the nursery's existing resources. Friendly conversation over the weeks is helping Clare to know more about the family. There is no expectation that Rafat's parents will be a source of information about the entire African continent. Their country of origin is Uganda and, furthermore, the family relocated to England when Rafat's parents were themselves young children.

Questions

1 Do you work in a neighbourhood with limited obvious ethnic group diversity? In what ways do you address the kind of issues faced by the Whittons team?

2 Are there views in your team that need to be challenged in a firm but professional way? Perhaps that families are asked whether they really want 'special' dolls or books for their children? Families who are very much in the minority locally would have to feel really self-assured to say 'Yes'. Perhaps they would feel that limited financial resources were being stretched just for them.

Take another **perspective**

Sometimes a team in a mainly White area will say that equality over ethnic group and culture is 'nothing to do with us'. Since the children do not apparently experience cultural variation, practitioners claim it should not affect resources or activities. If such feelings are strong in some of your team or childminding network, try the following exercise.

Find a map and draw a circle 20 miles in all directions around your setting or family home. Now, imagine that you have to remove anything from your centre or home that children could neither see nor hear within that circle.

- Are you within 20 miles of the sea? If not, then out go any books, jigsaws or pictures about the seaside, sea fishing or seagoing boats. And perhaps the sand tray should be removed as well.

- Take away any books and pictures showing animals or birds, unless children can see the real thing locally. The same goes for flowers, trees and shrubs.

- Remove anything that relates to castles, forts or palaces, unless you have a real one nearby.

- Remove any books, pictures, construction materials, play people or dressing-up clothes that reflect anything that children could not directly observe within the 20-mile boundary.

- And what if the children are not allowed to draw anything they could not observe in their own everyday lives?

You will probably not get far into the activity (making a list or an actual pile of resources) before somebody says that it is ridiculous to remove all these learning resources from children. Of course, it would be very foolish to organise a group setting or childminder's home in this way. Children's learning is seriously restricted if the only permitted sources of play and ideas are those that can be personally experienced locally. All children need resources and experiences that extend their understanding beyond their immediate daily life in ways that make sense to them.

Respect for cultural identity

Play and learning resources matter in every early years, school or out-of-school service. Your aim is to reflect the cultural traditions of children who attend your provision. Children, and their families, need to see themselves represented throughout resources and events. Children need to feel that they belong as individuals through those experiences that create their ethnic group and cultural identity. An equally important aim is to extend the horizons of all the children. So you will need to make some choices, but will not be restricted to cultural traditions represented locally.

All traditions should be approached with respect and it is important to avoid any implication that the main traditions within the current group are more 'normal' than the other 'exotic' or 'unusual' traditions that you explore briefly. This approach has sometimes been called a 'tourist curriculum' because the underlying message is that the experiences are not related to ordinary life. Whatever the background of individuals in your provision, practitioners are responsible for encouraging attitudes of respect as well as interest. It would be no more acceptable for a mainly African-Caribbean group of children to ridicule Japanese clothes or food than it would be to overlook such behaviour from a mainly White European group of children.

Underprivileged White ethnic/social groups

Early years practitioners are responsible for supporting a positive identity by cultural group for all the children. Written material about equality through resources has mostly focused on supporting the personal identity of children from minority ethnic groups. This emphasis has been understandable, given a past history of inadequacy of resources to reflect non-European traditions. However, the current generation of young children all need to develop a positive sense of history and culture for the group(s) to which they and their families belong.

Figure 4.2 Food is part of young children's family identity

Concern has been expressed about White UK children in socially deprived areas. Boys and girls may have no obvious sources of positive identity unless they are disdainful and rejecting of ethnic minority groups. This important issue for early years, school and out-of-school practitioners was raised in the 1990s by Barry Troyna (Connolly and Troyna, 1998; Troyna and Hatcher, 1992). Troyna's research has been quoted mostly in reference to the racist attitudes expressed by some pupils. The dynamic underlying some negative outlooks and the implications for building a positive identity for White children have been less discussed, until at least a decade later.

For a long time, the concept of addressing White ethnic group identity failed to connect with the prevailing framework of challenging racism. Resistance to considering this additional perspective linked with a belief that such views could be taken to excuse White children of racism, because their culture was undervalued. Best-quality practice needs to 'grasp the nettle' on this particular issue. This apt phrase is used in the C4EO (2010) review about early intervention with disadvantaged families. The C4EO message is that respect for family life has to coexist with honest appraisal that some parents are not meeting minimal standards for their children's well being and development.

At the time of writing, we are in the second decade of the 21st century. Grasping the nettle for race quality now definitely involves recognition that understanding the possible dynamics of disdain for others – especially in the case of children and young adolescents – is not the same as saying, 'OK, go ahead, then.' The school curriculum review by Keith Ajegbo et al. (2007) made a strong point that some White pupils had a negative perception of their own identity. It was a misplaced presumption that White pupils inevitably absorbed a positive sense of their own history, because their backgrounds had not been tainted with the legacy of racism. A responsible focus on the present, for disadvantaged White children and adolescents, means respectful attention to their sense of being marginalised.

Any equality approach has to be fully inclusive, and that means helping potentially disaffected White children. Some boys and girls really need to explore their own sources of personal, family and cultural identity in ways that boost their senses of self-worth, without bigoted feelings of superiority that desperately boil down to, 'At least I'm not a …'. Experiences and resources matter to help children of every ethnic group to establish a sense of positive identity and explore a shared history. Equality is not a competitive exercise and any concerns can be grounded in an overview of how all children are likely to gain a sense of pride in their origins.

Truly inclusive equality practice means weaving in an active appreciation of cultural, historical, linguistic and other sources of a personal identity rooted in the UK. Children have a right to develop a pride in being English, Welsh, Scottish or Irish. Even those divisions for identity have further meaning. As readers from Northern Ireland will know very well, a serious division between communities in that part of the UK falls between a wish to be seen as British or Irish.

If you want to find out more

- Ajegbo, K., Kiwan, D. and Sharma, S. (2007) *Diversity and Citizenship Curriculum Review*. London: DfES, **https://www.education.gov.uk/publications/standard/publicationdetail/page1/DFES-00045-2007** (accessed 5 September 2011).

- Barnard, H. and Turner, C. (2011) *Poverty and Ethnicity: A Review of the Evidence.* York: Joseph Rowntree Trust, **www.jrf.org.uk/publications/poverty-and-ethnicity-review-evidence**
- Equality and Human Rights Commission, **www.equalityhumanrights.com**
- C4EO (2010) *Grasping the Nettle: Early Intervention for Children, Families and Communities,* **www.c4eo.org.uk/themes/earlyintervention/default. aspx?themeid=12&accesstypeid=1** (accessed 5 September 2011).
- Connolly, P. (1998) *Racism, Gender Identities and Young Children: Social Relations in a Multi-Ethnic Inner-City School.* London: Routledge.
- Connolly, P. and Troyna, B. (eds) (1998) *Researching Racism in Education: Policies, Theory and Practice.* Buckingham: Open University Press.
- Gaine, C. (2005) *We're All White, Thanks: The Persisting Myth about White Schools.* Stoke-on-Trent: Trentham Books.
- Lane, J. (2008) *Young Children and Racial Justice.* London: National Children's Bureau.
- Milner, D. (1983) *Children and Race: Ten Years On.* London: Ward Lock Educational. (A useful summary of research up to the 1980s that provides an insight into social history.)
- Sveinsson, K.P. (ed) (2009) *Who Cares about the White Working Class.* London: Runnymede Trust, **www.runnymedetrust.org/uploads/publications/pdfs/ WhoCaresAboutTheWhiteWorkingClass-2009.pdf** (accessed 5 September 2011).
- Troyna, B. and Hatcher, R. (1992) *Racism in Children's Lives: A Study of Mainly White Primary Schools.* London: National Children's Bureau.
- Wright, C. (1992) *Race Relations in the Primary School.* London: Routledge.

Religious faith and personal beliefs

Family life and the raising of children can be influenced by parents' religious faith and by personal belief systems that matter a great deal but are not religious in origin. Identity by faith is often intermingled with ethnic group and cultural traditions. Some adults, and by association their children, prefer to identify themselves by faith than by ethnic group or nationality. (Look back at page 10 for definitions of terms.)

Ethnic monitoring is not straightforward, because people have clear and different preferences about how they wish to self-describe (see also page 15). Some UK residents are content to identify themselves as 'British Asian'. However, Asia is a large continent comprising different countries, languages, faiths and cultural traditions. Some people definitely wish to choose 'British Muslim' or 'British Hindu'. Distinctions and the sources of family ways can be less than obvious to people who are unfamiliar with the group. Ignorance, misunderstanding and stereotyping can also undermine or derail harmonious relationships across these group boundaries.

Negative blurring of boundaries worsens in times of social stress and fear, such as the London bombings of July 2005. Media reporting, let alone ordinary conversation, frequently muddles broad ethnicity, as in 'Asian', with faith, as in 'Muslim' – not to mention the untrue implication that all, or most, followers of Islam are 'extremist' or 'fundamentalist'. Aggressive reactions to events show evidence of this ignorance, stereotyping and failure to see diversity in a group to which writers or speakers do not themselves belong.

Faith and culture

Religious beliefs and practices have shaped societies around the world. When there has been a long history of a particular faith associated with a country, then religious practices become merged with the culture and can affect virtually every aspect of a society: social, moral and political. What was originally rooted in religious faith becomes seen as 'normal' life. Habits are absorbed into everyday language, expected ways of behaving and celebrations by people who are no longer active members of the particular religious faith.

Additionally, faiths like Christianity, Buddhism or Islam have spread far beyond their historical roots. Versions of the main faith have developed varied cultural traditions in the details of religious observance or applications to daily life. For example, modest dress is a requirement within Islam, for both men and women. The detailed interpretation of modesty in dress and demeanour for women has evolved in diverse ways for different communities around the world. Only some communities within this widespread faith regard it as obligatory for women to cover their entire face and hands.

The UK as an example

The four nations of the UK have a long history of being shaped by Christianity. The faith arrived in the fifth century, most likely brought by St Patrick to Ireland, and steadily gained followers, absorbing some of the pre-existing Celtic beliefs. A major schism was provoked by Henry VIII in the 16th century, when he broke from the religious leadership of the Pope in Rome. An alternative denomination of Christianity developed in England, known as Protestant to be distinguished from Catholic. The Church of England became the established church and the monarch retains the title Defender of the Faith.

Throughout the 20th century, being 'C of E' was regarded by many people as much the same as being 'English': a sense of being nominally Christian unless you said to the contrary. There are different denominations within Christianity and England is not the only country in the UK. I recall as a child visiting the Welsh half of my family and being kindly corrected by my grandmother, who explained that in the valleys people did not go to church, they went to chapel. The Church of England was the English faith and the local community was Welsh Methodist by tradition. The Scottish Presbyterian Church also has distinct practices.

Scenarios

The merging of religious and cultural tradition is relevant for practitioners. Even adults who no longer practise the faith in which they were raised often prefer to follow patterns established in their own childhood.

1

At Crest Road Early Years Centre, Chloe and her mother are keen to show staff some photos of the new baby's christening. This conversation is the first time either parent has mentioned the Christian faith. They are not regular churchgoers, but feel more comfortable having baby Jessica christened.

2

When Aaron and his parents first visited the Whittons Nursery, they explained that Aaron was not to be given any pork or shellfish. Clare, the manager, commented that there was no synagogue in the town and it became clear that Aaron's family was not active in the Jewish faith. His parents simply preferred to follow the diet in which they had been raised.

Questions

1 In each setting the comments and requests from parents were taken seriously. In Chloe's case an important family event was shared and in Aaron's case the request about diet was respected.

2 Have similar situations arisen within your own setting or service as a childminder?

Take another **perspective**

If your childhood was spent in the UK, or another culture strongly influenced by Christianity, you may never have questioned a feeling that it is normal to believe in one god (monotheism) and that religions that have more than one deity are therefore unusual, even a bit strange.

I recall working with an early years team that was very diverse by ethnic group, but most of the team had a Christian background, even if they were no longer active. Conversation turned to Hinduism during one session and several people turned to their only Indian colleague to say with great surprise, 'But you don't believe in reincarnation, do you?' She replied, 'Of course I do.' The group clearly had to adjust to the experience that a fellow practitioner, who was very much 'one of us', believed in an idea that most of the team had learned was out of the ordinary.

Diversity within faiths

Six main world faiths are often featured most prominently within supporting materials for early years, school and playwork professionals.

1 Hinduism is the oldest major world faith, established about 5,000 years ago in India. The specific name dates from about 800 years ago, when followers were identified as Hindu, the Persian word for Indian.

2 Judaism has existed for about 3,500 years and developed in the area known from a European perspective as the Middle East. It is the first faith known to be monotheistic (belief in a single deity).

3 Buddhism stretches back some 2,500 years to its origins in India, where it was founded by Gautama, who became the Buddha, meaning 'The Enlightened One'.

4 Christianity evolved about 2,000 years ago in part of the Middle East then known as Palestine. Believers worship one god whom they believe created the world and took human form as Jesus Christ (the Messiah).

5 Islam emerged as a world faith, in what is now Saudi Arabia, about 1,400 years ago, led by the Prophet Muhammad (always said with the additional Arabic phrase meaning 'peace and blessings of Allah upon him').

6 Sikhism developed over 500 years ago within the Punjab (an area stretching from what became Pakistan into north-west India). The movement was started by Guru Nanak.

All the faiths spread beyond their point of origin, sometimes because of population movements. However, some followers deliberately travelled to other countries in order to convert members of that population. World faiths have developed variations in different locations. Sometimes followers have absorbed the practices of pre-existing religions in the culture. Buddhism in India differs from the faith in Japan, because the latter developed in coexistence with Shintoism, an ancient religion based in animist beliefs of a supernatural force within all natural objects. Differences also arise because of unresolved divisions within the faith. The Orthodox Church in eastern Europe split over questions of belief long before the schism that divided Protestant from Catholic Christianity in western Europe.

You will be aware of sects within the world faith most familiar to you. However, diversity is a feature of every major world faith. There is disagreement, sometimes significant, over core beliefs, interpretations of the main holy book(s), the details of daily practice like diet or dress, aspects of worship and related cultural tradition. For no faith can you confidently say 'Everyone believes that ...' or 'Everyone behaves in this way.' It is also unjust to generalise from the behaviour of the more uncompromising groups, in any faith, to claim that intolerance is an integral part of that religion.

Disagreements can turn vicious between followers of different faiths – for example, the continuing violence between some Hindus and some Muslims in India. Some of the massacres that occurred through the early 1990s in the former Yugoslavia were determined along Christian–Muslim divisions, sometimes between people who had coexisted as neighbours for decades. However, the sectarian divisions between the Protestant and Catholic denominations of Christianity in Northern Ireland are thoroughly entangled with historical, political and social factors. The resulting ill feeling, violence and social disturbance have disrupted generations.

Uncompromising versions of a faith are sometimes called fundamentalist. The term seemed first to arise from Christian sects that took the Bible as literal truth. In contrast, other Christians regard the Old and New Testaments as more symbolic and open to different interpretations. The term fundamentalist has increasingly been used to mean a follower of any faith whose allegiance involves rejection of everyone who does not agree with their faith or with this specific version. The word is sometimes applied indiscriminately to followers of Islam; this is unacceptable. Muslims are not all fundamentalists in this sense, any more than the allegation can legitimately be made of all Christians.

Diversity of faith in the UK

For many centuries the different denominations of Christianity were by far the most prominent faith in the UK. However, Judaism has been present for many centuries because there were Jewish communities in many cities. These settlements experienced periodic violence and persecution as a direct result of their faith. Other sources of religious diversity mainly developed with the population movements of the 20th century.

Many migrants from the Caribbean and the African continent were active Christians or, like other residents of the UK, shared that faith as a cultural backdrop to daily life. Migrants from some countries in Africa, Asia and Malaysia followed Islam. Some migrants and refugees from parts of Europe, are also Muslim. Migrants from the Punjab are frequently Sikh by faith. Buddhism is a widely dispersed faith and followers may originate from many parts of the world, not only from India or China. Through the 1960s and 1970s some UK residents became intrigued by eastern mysticism and became committed to the faith.

Faith and professional practice

Knowledge and understanding

Early years practitioners are not expected to be experts on religion. Your responsibility for equality practice is to be aware of the gaps in what you know and be ready to learn more. You should also be willing to check your understanding, even when colleagues share the same assumptions. You may all have misunderstood the real significance of a religious festival or the reason for particular practices. There is no shame in admitting to confusion or having misunderstood. It is, however, unprofessional if practitioners shut their mind to that possibility.

If you keep an open mind, you will extend your learning about faiths that are unfamiliar to you, but you are also likely to learn more about the religious faith that is most familiar, perhaps a faith in which you were raised or which you still practise. It can be hard to stand back from beliefs that seem part of everyday life, and it can be valuable to grasp finally, 'Oh, that's why we do that!' This opportunity to continue to learn applies whatever the faith that is most familiar to you.

Respect and belief

You will not be in tune with everyone over religious faith or personal belief systems. You are not expected to agree, or pretend to agree, with every colleague or parent who expresses their personal beliefs. Best practice includes the following:

- Having a clear policy that includes matters of faith within how you address equality in your daily practice.
- Creating opportunities to discuss within a team any confusion or disagreement that arises through conversations with parents, or indeed from diversity of belief within the team. Childminders benefit from being part of a local network and having easy contact with local support advisors.
- Acknowledging differences and showing respect for beliefs and practices that you may not share. Respect applies regardless of whether you currently have contact with a family that follows the faith in question.
- Showing respect through an active attempt to understand any requests that parents make based on religious or other personal beliefs. If the setting genuinely cannot meet parents' requests, then you should be honest and seek a compromise, if possible.

Mutual respect

The way in which you approach experiences within your practice should demonstrate that you value faiths equally. Nobody should behave in their professional life as if one religion is more important or true than any other.

Practitioners and policy makers are sometimes concerned that offence will be given to followers of one faith by the sheer presence of celebrations or symbols linked with another faith. It is important to be aware of the significance of events or symbols, and to ensure that the resources and experiences you offer children are balanced. Such sensitivity is a significant part of equality practice in Northern Ireland, which addresses sectarianism. Young children in that part of the UK become aware of how flags, sporting allegiance and events like marches carry symbolic meaning for Catholic and Protestant sects (Connolly et al., 2002).

Part of religious faith for some followers is that they are definitely right and anyone who does not share their beliefs, or this version of the faith, is definitely wrong. This evaluative judgement is not necessarily hostile to non-believers. Indeed, the conviction leads some faith members towards active attempts to convert other people: an evangelical stance. However, some sects within different world faiths are more dogmatic than others and some are utterly rejecting of outsiders, as well as of any divergence of opinion within the same faith. This situation can shock people unfamiliar with the group beliefs and complicates good practice on equality. Respect for anyone's beliefs has to be balanced with an awareness that nobody is to impose their beliefs on colleagues, parents or children in the service or setting.

Personal beliefs and spirituality

Policy and practice on equality over faith must also recognise that parents who do not actively follow a particular faith can still have strong beliefs about how to behave and raise their children. It is disrespectful to assume that families with no specific religious beliefs lack moral values to guide their decisions. The Equality Act 2010 (see page 21) explicitly recognises that beliefs should be actively respected, whether or not these are part of an established religion.

If people have religious beliefs, then their sense of spirituality is very likely to be interwoven with their faith. However, 'religious' is not inevitably the same as 'spiritual'. It is possible and appropriate to address the spiritual aspect of children's development through awareness of human experience that does not have to answer to rational analysis. Whatever the family faith or belief system, children can be encouraged in a sense of wonder, often through enchantment about the natural world, and peaceful contemplation.

Religious affiliation

If a group setting has no definite religious affiliation, then any parent, practitioner or volunteer needs to understand policy and practice on equality. Adults have the right to their own beliefs, and team members will show respect, including flexibility in connection with requests arising from religious practice.

However, rights are accompanied by the responsibility to show respect in their turn and no practitioner should tell children that only this single faith or sect is true. The early years frameworks around the UK are consistent in promoting mutual respect and avoiding any specific religious allegiance. Childminders who have committed to a particular religion may have symbols of their faith within the home. It would be expected that, whatever the faith, practitioners would not push forward their beliefs. In your own home, as in any group setting, it is appropriate to answer any questions or comments put by children themselves.

Some early years settings are linked with a specific place of worship and therefore religious faith or denomination. The situation must be made clear in the brochure or other form of written material about the setting. Registered early years settings and providers are still obliged to show respect for religions in addition to the faith followed by staff.

Religious education is a feature of the school curriculum throughout the UK. Use of the term 'education' rather than 'religious instruction' reflects the focus that it is a teacher's role to educate children about faith in general and not to instruct them in specific religious beliefs or practices. Schools are expected to organise a regular experience of collective worship of a broadly Christian nature unless the school has been given permission to vary this format (usually because a significant proportion of pupils follow another world faith).

The general approach is that children will experience this part of the curriculum together and not be subdivided by belief. Parents have the right to withdraw their children from RE or the collective worship. Faith schools may offer, separately, to organise specific religious instruction in preparation for events such as confirmation, a ceremony of personal dedication to faith for some Christian denominations.

In England, Wales and Scotland the majority of state schools do not have a specific religious affiliation. Most faith schools have allegiance to Protestant (Church of England) or Catholic denominations of Christianity. There are a small number of Jewish schools and a few Muslim and Sikh schools. The situation is reversed in Northern Ireland, where most schools are affiliated along Christian denominational lines: Protestant or Catholic. Since the 1980s the National Ireland Integrated Education Movement has pressed for settings that are not restricted to one sect (**www.nicie.org/**).

If you want to find out more

- Bull, P. (2006) 'Shifting patterns of social identity in Northern Ireland', *The Psychologist,* 19, 1, 40–43, **www.thepsychologist.org.uk/archive/archive_home.cfm ?volumeID=19&editionID=131&ArticleID=976**
- Community Relations Council (Northern Ireland) material explaining an anti-sectarian approach, **www.community-relations.org.uk** (accessed 27 July 2011).
- Connolly, P., Smith, A. and Kelly, B. (2002) *Too Young to Notice: The Cultural and Political Awareness of 3–6 Year Olds in Northern Ireland.* Belfast: Community Relations Council.
- Learning and Teaching Scotland, **www.ltscotland.org.uk/antisectarian** (accessed 27 July 2011).
- Lindon, J. (1999) *Understanding World Religions in Early Years Practice.* London: Hodder and Stoughton.
- Qualifications and Curriculum Authority (QCA), *Religious Education: Glossary of Terms,* **www.qca.org.uk/downloads/6148_re_glossary.pdf** (accessed 27 July 2011).
- Smith, G. (2005) *Children's Perspectives on Believing and Belonging.* York: Joseph Rowntree Trust, **www.jrf.org.uk/publications/childrens-perspectives-believing-and-belonging**

Disability and health

Some children cope with the difference made to daily life by learning, physical or emotional disabilities, or a continuing health condition that leaves them feeling ill on a regular or permanent basis. Equality practice over disability has much in common with other aspects of inclusion. However, like gender, ethnic group and faith, there are some issues that benefit from a separate discussion. Disabled children should be seen and recognised as children, not viewed only through their disability or health condition, and practitioners need to explore how to manage that aim.

The main sections of this chapter cover:
- the range of disability and chronic ill health
- disabled children in society
- special support for disabled children.

The range of disability and chronic ill health

Early years practitioners are not expected to know about every possible health condition or disability that you might encounter within your entire career. Furthermore, new research and reviews of practice often mean that the information and advice of ten, or even five, years ago is overtaken. A realistic approach and best practice are for everyone to be:
- willing to find out, to listen and to learn – from parents, the children themselves, other professionals and the many organisations that are keen to inform and advise
- ready to consider your expectations for disabled children and to consider your assumptions – some may be inaccurate and unhelpful.

There are many different kinds of disability and the aim of this section is to give you a sense of the range. A website reference is given the first time each condition is mentioned. Details of further resources can be found on page 91.

Physical disabilities

Some children are mainly or wholly physically disabled and the effect may be anything from mild to very severe. Here are some examples.
- Muscular dystrophy is a progressive disease in which children's muscles waste away. There are variations of the condition, but Duchenne is the form more commonly identified within early childhood and directly affects only boys (**www.muscular-dystrophy.org**).
- Children who are blind or deaf live with a disability of the senses that affects the way in which they learn in other areas of development. Children learn to

or the health visitor. These people, however knowledgeable, may be far less well known to the family than their key person or childminder.

Early years settings are required to have a written Special Educational Needs (SEN) policy, which makes clear the obligation for equality practice. There must be a designated member of staff with lead responsibility for SEN. This named team member, often called the special educational needs coordinator (SENCO), offers support to the team. Their additional expertise is not used to take over from the key person, but to support that existing relationship with the family. The SENCO would usually liaise with other professionals and also ensure continued professional development for the team on disability issues.

Being proactive for inclusion

The law does not require settings or childminders to run up huge bills for structural alterations to buildings. However, a nursery or school – and, within reasonable limits, the childminding services – is required to look ahead – for instance, in anticipating the needs of children or parents who use wheelchairs or other mobility aids. It is not an acceptable excuse to say that no child or parent currently involved with the provision has serious mobility problems.

It is good practice for settings or childminders to consider how they would adjust to the needs of a child with profound hearing loss or whose behaviour fell within the autistic spectrum. In contrast, it would be unacceptable for any practitioner or team simply to refuse children in the belief that their health or learning needs will be 'too difficult' or that other children or their parents allegedly 'wouldn't like it'.

You may doubt your ability to provide for a child. The legal obligation to work for inclusion does not say that all early years providers must be ready to accept any individual, profoundly disabled or chronically ill child. Some special needs, which are daily needs for this child, may be genuinely beyond your capacity to meet. Professionalism in equality practice is met by serious consideration and reasonable adjustments. If your answer has to be a regretful, 'I'm sorry,' then you show respect with an explanation, based on the child's needs, the limitations of your premises or practical details of the service the family needs.

The requirements from laws against disability discrimination mean that some managers and their teams have had to revisit unreasonable rules such as 'We don't give medicines here' or 'All children must be toilet trained.' For some children daily medication is part of normal life, not temporary illness for which 'They should be at home.' Some children with disabilities will take longer to attain self-care skills; some may always need considerable help (more in Chapter 6.)

Disabled children have the right to enjoy all the events and resources within early years, school or out-of-school provision. It is unacceptable for practitioners simply to decide to exclude a child from an activity or an outing because the adult thinks inclusion will be 'too much trouble'. Such actions are discriminatory and therefore illegal. The main aim of the laws and related guidance documents is to encourage a 'can-do' outlook.

Figure 5.2 All children sometimes need special attention

Practitioners need to be ready and able to access advice in order to ensure that they are confident in dealing with a child's daily health issues. Teams may need support to find ways to include children fully in activities that look problematic at the outset, or provoke adult anxiety about children's safety. Children whose behaviour is very unpredictable may not be safe on an outing unless an adult can be assigned to them on a one-to-one basis. However, the longer-term plan needs to be to bring children alongside the adult effort and, within the scope of children's understanding, to enable them to understand the consequences of their actions.

Inclusion is a continuing process that depends on alert adult observation and listening to the views of the children themselves. They are the best judges of whether they feel welcome and an easy partner in experiences. Disabled children need to feel able to make genuine choices within their play and, of course, that will sometimes mean declining an invitation to join an activity. Practitioners need to get to know any disabled children as individuals and build partnership with their families. Of course, disabled children still all have their own unique temperaments and it is important to avoid stereotypes.

Disability – a Consultation (**www.education.gov.uk/childrenandyoungpeople/ sen/a0075339/sengreenpaper**). See also Department for Education *Early Support* programme for children and families (**www.education.gov.uk/ childrenandyoungpeople/sen/earlysupport**).

In Scotland, The *Supporting Children's Learning: Code of Practice* applies. Special educational needs are now addressed within the broader context of 'Additional Support for Learning' (**www.scotland.gov.uk/ Publications/2005/08/15105817/58187**).

The Welsh Assembly has promoted use of the descriptive phrase 'additional learning needs' (ALN). Practitioners in Wales should consult the *Special Educational Needs Code of Practice for Wales* (2004) (**http://wales.gov.uk/topics/ educationandskills/publications/guidance/specialeduneedscop/?lang=en**).

In Northern Ireland you should consult the *Disability Discrimination Code of Practice for Schools* (**www.equalityni.org/archive/pdf/FSchoolsCOP(SENDO).pdf**).

Building a relationship with disabled children

Unfortunately, some people still, when they look at a disabled child, see the condition rather than the child. Good practice in early years, in schools and out-of-school provision is to develop a personal, positive relationship with a disabled child – as you should with any children who are your responsibility. This important relationship is led through the key person approach, which should be common to best practice with all children and families (Lindon, 2010).

Practitioners always need to learn what the disability or health condition means for this child. You then put your more general knowledge into practice within the context of working with individual children and their families.

- As a childminder, you set the tone for your home in terms of language. In a group setting, team leaders need to ensure that all staff, including any volunteers or parent helpers, relate to children as individuals.
- Practitioners can have empathy for and appreciation of children's frustrations, but avoid pity, either through sad looks or comments such as 'Poor little Louisa – if only she could talk properly.' Have a private, although firm, conversation with any student or volunteer who talks in this way.
- It is positive to explain that 'Joshua has cerebral palsy' rather than use phrases like 'He suffers from cerebral palsy.' You are not pretending that cerebral palsy is a condition that anyone would choose to have. However, the way you talk about Joshua should leave nobody surprised that he has a passion for dinosaurs and a wicked sense of humour.
- Children should never be described just by their disability or health condition. This approach is disrespectful and chips away at children's individuality. It would be discourteous to say of children, 'Megan is our little Down's' or 'You know Alric – the epileptic.'

Scenario

Social relationships can take more careful building with children with autistic spectrum disorders. The world is a different place for four-year-old Max who has attended the Whittons Nursery over the last year.

Max's level of understanding is very literal. He is puzzled by the subtleties communicated by exactly how something is said or the social conventions of play that his peers have now learned. Max has needed a lot of personal support from Janice, his key person, in order to feel at ease with the nursery routine. He needs warning of any changes, because he experiences even minor disruptions as scary.

It has been important that Janice and her colleagues understand that children like Max can develop very rigid personal routines and play preferences in order to cope with anxiety and unpredictability. Janice, in close partnership with Max's father, has helped the young boy to begin to understand some of the non-verbal cues in play and to manage basic social skills. Max is still often perplexed by what is a joke and what is serious, as well as many aspects of pretend play.

Comments

Children can be very straightforward about disabled peers, but they still want an atmosphere of fairness. Three- and four-year-olds get very annoyed if 'being special' means a child is allowed to break important rules.

It is easy to take for granted the subtle social skills gained by most four-year-olds until you tune in to the struggles of children with autistic spectrum disorder. When you observe how a child unwittingly breaks the social rules of play, you realise how shared social assumptions underpin rich play between young children.

Find out more from the National Autistic Society (**www.nas.org.uk**), which has direct information and suggestions for books and stories.

If you want to find out more

- Advisory Centre for Education has information about state-funded education for England and Wales. **www.ace-ed.org.uk**
- Casey, T. (2010) *Inclusive Play: Practical Strategies for Children from Birth to Eight.* London: Sage Publications.
- Council for Disabled Children. **www.ncb.org.uk/cdc**
- Department for Children, Schools and Families (2008) *Inclusion Development Programme: Supporting Children with Speech, Language and Communication Needs,* **https://www.education.gov.uk/publications/eOrderingDownload/pr_idp_eyfs_0021508.pdf**
- Department for Children, Schools and Families (2009) *Inclusion Development Programme: Supporting Children on the Autistic Spectrum,* **www.education.gov.uk/publications/eOrderingDownload/idp_eyfs_autism_guide.pdf**
- Department of Education – Northern Ireland. **www.deni.gov.uk**
- Drifte, C. (2008) *Encouraging Positive Behaviour in the Early Years.* London: Sage.
- Hemihelp. **www.hemihelp.org.uk**
- Leaman, L. (2005) *Managing Very Challenging Behaviour.* London: Continuum.

practitioners take equivalent care with hats, sun protection cream and drinking water for everyone.

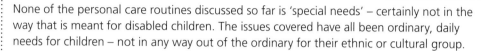

Pause for reflection

None of the personal care routines discussed so far is 'special needs' – certainly not in the way that is meant for disabled children. The issues covered have all been ordinary, daily needs for children – not in any way out of the ordinary for their ethnic or cultural group.

Reflect on views you have heard in your team, or perhaps in the local childminding network. Practitioners are unlikely to intend to be discourteous, or inaccurate. But attention to skin or hair care only seems 'special' if practitioners lack experience.

Differences in colouration

Some children, from a range of ethnic groups, have areas that are without melanin and so have no pigmentation. This condition is called vitiligo and may not be noticed in lighter-skinned children until they are out in the sun. The permanently pale areas of skin are more noticeable when children otherwise have a dark skin colour. Vitiligo is not in itself a problem for health, except that children's skin needs to be protected by sun block. These affected areas of the body do not tan at all and sunburn swiftly results. Children may, however, feel very self-conscious, when the different skin tones are obvious (see www.vitiligosociety.org.uk).

Children of African-Caribbean, Asian and Mediterranean origin sometimes have patches of darker skin that occur naturally. Historically, this condition has been called 'Mongolian blue spots'. Families and health workers fairly object to this phrase, because it arises from classifying children and families as being of the 'Mongoloid race'. The medical term is congenital dermal melanocytosis.

The darker areas are benign skin markings, but unfortunately can look, to the inexperienced eye, like bruising. These areas are a consistent slate blue in colour, unlike genuine bruising that varies in shade and changes over a period of days. However, the similarity has sometimes raised concerns of non-accidental injury. Good practice in child protection would always include a careful conversation with children and their parents. An open-ended approach will give children, and their parents, the opportunity to tell you that these differences in skin colouration are permanent.

Modest clothing and hair coverings

Some faiths have requirements about clothing that arise from considerations of modesty and religious and/or cultural tradition. As in any faith, some families will be stricter about their children's dress code than others. Problems arise if practitioners are insensitive to arrangements, when children need to change their clothes, perhaps for special physical activities or for the swimming lessons.

You should be ready to consider children's dignity and desire for privacy, regardless of whether specific religious views have been expressed. Generally kind adults can be insensitive about young children's feelings, thinking they will never mind communal changing rooms, or even changing in a primary school corridor. The very youngest children may not give a hoot but some four- and five-year-olds start to expect a level of privacy. Children who live with skin conditions such as eczema or vitiligo can feel very self-conscious about undressing to reveal limbs. Those emotions are heightened if other children have made offhand or rude remarks. The same issue can arise for children who already have a serious problem of being overweight. Respectful and good practice is to ensure that all children have options and nobody is made to feel 'silly' or that they are 'making a fuss about nothing'.

Several faiths have traditions that affect clothing and covering the hair. Muslim families, for instance, are likely to be concerned that girls in particular keep to modest styles of dress. However, families that follow Islam, like any other world faith, vary in how strictly they wish to follow codes of daily practice. The basic requirement from the Qur'an is for modest dress for both sexes. Different cultural traditions of clothing have arisen in Muslim communities from different parts of the world, so the aim of modesty is achieved by different kinds of head covering and overall clothing. Some groups are considerably more concerned about female than male forms of dress and the issues usually become more acute for older girls and adolescents.

However, Islam is not the only faith in which beliefs affect styles of dress.
- Some Jewish and Christian groups require women and girls to keep their head covered by a scarf, although all the hair may not have to be enclosed. Families are often equally concerned about appropriate dress for boys, although people outside the group may be more alert to requirements for girls.
- Jewish boys may wear a kippah, the small cap-type hat that covers the top of their head. Males wear a kippah during prayers, but some groups like the boys to wear it all the time.
- Rastafarian parents may ask that their daughters keep their hair neatly covered by a scarf and the sons with a hat in rasta colours (called a tam), which contains their dreadlocks. Strict Rastafarians neither cut nor comb their hair, which then twists naturally to form the dreadlocks.
- Sikhs do not cut their hair – neither females nor males. Girls and women will have different ways of styling their long hair. Young boys have the hair plaited neatly around their head. When they are older, boys' hair is wound into a close circular style on top of the head (jura) contained by a small cloth covering (patka). Male adolescents will eventually have a turban.

Religious symbols
Children may sometimes wear items that have religious significance. Good practice is to ask parents and certainly not to insist on removal of an item just

Figure 6.1 Children enjoy helping with real domestic tasks

The cultural, religious and linguistic background of refugee families will, of course, vary, because they come from different parts of the world. Families may also have a home language other than English and so their children may be learning English as their second or third language. The routine and approach of an early years setting or a primary school may be anything from slightly to extremely unfamiliar to the children. The exact situation will depend on their country of origin and children's experiences prior to relocation. The additional issue to consider is that families who are refugees from their country of origin may have left under distressing or dangerous circumstances. Asylum seekers live with uncertainty over whether they will be given refugee status and permitted to stay in the UK. This situation adds to unfamiliarity to mean that children and their parents need that much more support.

Scenario

St Agnes Pre-school has a mix of Gypsy and Traveller children along with children of settled families. The team avoids assumptions, but has learned that the settling-in process can be harder for Gypsy and Traveller children than even the most cautious children from settled families. Some children have not previously experienced such a large indoor space, with the number of people and lively activities that are usual for a session at St Agnes.

Michelle and her team have looked at use of space and better use of their outdoor area, and have found that the changes have benefited many of the children. Not all Gypsy and Traveller children have been continuously on the road; some families have lived on the local site for years. However, other Gypsy children had limited experience with the sinks and flush toilets that their peers took for granted.

Comments

Some Gypsy and Traveller children will have experienced an early years setting. But, for others, the early days on a primary school site will be their very first time in a non-home environment with many strangers. If you work in a reception class you may assume that all children will have been to nursery or pre-school because so many under-fives now have this experience.

Male and female practitioners

Some families feel strongly that females should undertake all the personal care of young children, especially girls. Such an outlook may create an impasse over male practitioners as childminders or members of a mixed-sex team.

These feelings may arise from cultural tradition and habit – a belief that females are more caring or the only appropriate carers for very young children. The rationale may also be supported by particular religious beliefs. However, some reluctance to trust male practitioners has been fuelled in more recent years by anxiety over child protection and misrepresentations about the risk of abuse to children.

If parents express reservations over male practitioners then a team, or local advisor, has to face the dilemma arising from two equally important sources of equality practice.

1 Respect for family preference based on faith or cultural tradition means that you should listen to and understand the source of reservations about a male key person.

2 However, equality on gender and legal implications for equal opportunities in employment are clear that male practitioners should fulfil all responsibilities of the job, unless there is a non-discriminatory basis to creating differences in role.

As a team or a service, it is preferable that you think through this dilemma before you are faced with a real parent saying the words. You need to be clear on your policy stance and the reasons for your choice, and be able to express that simply to families. I believe that the best option, expressed honestly to parents, is that all practitioners are treated equally and expected to cover the same role (the choice made in the following scenario). This option also seems to be consistent with equality legislation, although I have not been successful in finding a clear statement on the issue in any guidance. (Recall the statement on page v that nowhere does this book offer legal advice.)

Scenario

Darren works with Maddie in the under-twos room of Crest Road Early Years Centre. A year ago Kitty's mother objected to Darren on the grounds that 'Everyone knows men can be abusers.' Liz, the centre manager, supported Darren as they worked through the issues with this family. The consistent message was that the problem would not be resolved by promising Darren would never change Kitty. The family decided nevertheless to accept the place and developed a friendly relationship with Darren.

Razia started with the centre this week and Darren is her key person. Today Razia's mother says to Liz that they had no idea Darren would do the personal care for their toddler. Razia's parents have strong views, based in their cultural background and Muslim faith, that only females should undertake personal care of babies. The family say they want Maddie to be Razia's key person.

Choice point: Liz has two main options here and both have consequences.

Option one

Liz decides that the faith basis of the objection to Darren is sufficient to agree that Razia will become a key child for Maddie and only female practitioners will undertake her personal care. However, this decision sets a precedent that gender equality is less important than preference based on faith, or beliefs reflecting cultural tradition. It is very likely that events will travel the parent grapevine and Kitty's parents will feel with hindsight that their concerns were not shown proper respect.

Pause, rewind to the choice point ...

Liz takes the second way out of this dilemma.

Option two

Liz apologises that the full implications of a key person approach had not come across clearly to Razia's parents. Liz explains that all practitioners share the same job description. In this room, Darren would be the back-up key person, if he were not the main contact for a family. She expresses respect for the family preference, but explains that, if exclusively female care is non-negotiable for Razia, then Crest Road will not meet the family's needs. Razia's mother looks doubtful, so Liz talks about childminding as a way to ensure a sole female carer, if the family requires this care.

Questions

1 Discuss the two options outlined in the scenario. How do you feel about each possibility?

2 Explore the dilemma with colleagues or fellow students.

Food and mealtimes

Early partnership with parents should always include a conversation about children's food preferences and full communication about any foods or drinks that need to be avoided.

EQUALITY AND INCLUSION IN EARLY CHILDHOOD

Different ways to a healthy diet

Any requests from families about food and drink for their children should be handled with equal respect, whatever the reason for asking. In a group setting the requests must be communicated to all team members who will have contact with children. Good patterns of communication can be especially important in schools where teachers may have the conversation with parents, yet different staff supervise mealtimes.

- Some children have allergies, occasionally severe, to certain food or ingredients found in home-made as well as processed meals.
- Some continuing health conditions arise from, or lead to, children's inability to eat or digest certain foods or drinks.
- Some families will request that their children are not given particular food or drink, because these are unacceptable for religious or cultural reasons.
- Some families follow a particular dietary option, such as being vegetarian or vegan, out of personal choice.

Pause for reflection

In your setting, how do you ensure clear communication about the dietary needs of individual children?

The information should be very clear in a child's personal folder and well understood by the key person. However, that practitioner will not always be present and you need a consistent way of checking each snack or meal.

Information should be easily available but not displayed in such a public way that any parent or visitor can read personal details about a child or family. How do you find a workable middle course?

A number of world faiths have a tradition of giving thanks for food, either at most mealtimes or on specific occasions. Childminders in their home or a group team may also have a tradition of showing appreciation for food. The form of thanks needs to be general, or enable children to express appreciation with a variety of words or gestures. It should not, for instance, be an exclusively Christian 'saying grace'.

Food preferences and traditions vary considerably and it would be unacceptable for any practitioners to take the line that their own cultural tradition is the normal way of eating and any variation is evidence of 'oddness'. Neither is it accurate to describe religious or personal food preferences as a 'restricted diet', solely because a family chooses not to eat a food that this practitioner considers to be 'normal'. Children could accurately be said to have restrictions on their diet when they are unable to eat foods, for health reasons, that would otherwise be on the family menu.

Pause for reflection

Many adults raised in the UK were given a hard time about 'Don't eat with your fingers! It's dirty!' So they unthinkingly repeat these words to children for whom they are now the responsible adult.

If this phrase pops out of your mouth, give it some thinking time. Hygiene is an important habit for children to learn: hand washing before food preparation as well as eating. Properly washed fingers and hands are not 'dirty'; they can be safer for health than inadequately cleaned cutlery.

Babies and children should experience enjoyable, social snack- and mealtimes. Mid-morning or mid-afternoon snacks can be more informal, perhaps with a rolling snack time for children to choose when to sit at the snack table with their friends. Lunchtimes benefit from sitting down together, although within a layout that offers small tables, and a welcome to children to help within the routine.

In your group you may have a range of dietary needs, and it may be very important that some children are given the correct plate or bowl of food. However, this responsibility can be met in ways that do not segregate children into different groups by their diet. Apart from the fact that children like to choose their mealtime companions, they learn about differences by understanding that their friend does not eat pork sausages or that another child needs to have the 'special' biscuits.

Scenario

Children learn habits about how to deal with food they do not want or like. Practitioners need to recognise that habits that are unacceptable to them may be normal practice for the child's family.

The team at St Agnes Pre-school have come to recognise that Gypsy and Traveller families are a diverse grouping. They have learned that some boys from Gypsy families, though certainly not all, throw disliked food on the ground. The boys are copying the behaviour of their father and other males, who discard food they do not like when they are working outdoors. What works fine in a field causes disruption indoors. The staff are ready to show that they understand the habit and yet they still guide children over 'what we all do here, if you really don't like your sandwich'.

Nevertheless, children's behaviour at mealtimes is not always rooted in a family cultural tradition. In Crest Road Early Years Centre, staff became aware that Manisha hid unwanted bits of food under the vegetable serving dish. A gentle conversation brought out that Manisha had developed this tactic at home to sidestep her gran, who gets very dramatic if anything is left on the plate. Manisha's behaviour had nothing to do with the family's faith or culture and everything to do with her gran's attitude towards food.

Comments

> Early years practitioners need to extend their knowledge of traditions that are less familiar at the outset. However, understanding and respect can go hand in hand with kindly guidance about 'what we do here'.
>
> Additionally, you never switch off your skills of observation and thinking as you make sense of the actions of individual children.

Faith and food choices

Some general guidelines follow, but please recall that there is a great deal of variety within every faith. You will always need to give time for a conversation with parents and children, when they are old enough, for clear explanations and practical detail about how a particular family operates.

- Buddhists are sometimes vegetarian, but not always. As for any children who are vegetarian, you need to get into the habit of checking the ingredients of processed and convenience foods. Unless marked as suitable for vegetarians, some products include animal-derived ingredients, such as gelatine or rennet. There are vegetarian alternatives to both these items. Some cheap ice creams include animal fat.
- Most Christians do not follow particular rules for their diet, although some make a case against vegetarianism by quoting the Bible. However, a few Christian groups avoid certain foods. Jehovah's Witnesses require that meat has been bled in the method of slaughter and avoid foods such as black pudding because of the blood. Some Rastafarians follow a vegetarian diet close to vegan, avoiding dairy products. If these families eat meat, they will probably avoid pork and shellfish. The Rastafarian faith is a blend of Biblical teachings and African (mainly Ethiopian) cultural traditions.
- Some Hindus are vegetarian, but those who eat meat will avoid any beef and beef products, since cows are regarded as sacred.
- In Judaism, the laws of Kashrut determine the foods that can be eaten and those that are forbidden. Meat and poultry must be obtained from kosher (meaning allowed) butchers to ensure the accepted method of killing animals and that meat has been blessed by the rabbi. Meat and dairy products have to be kept separate at all stages of food preparation, serving and eating and in washing-up afterwards. Unless you have a kitchen organised along kosher lines, children need to bring a packed lunch and utensils from home. Less strict Jewish families will ask that their children are not given pork and probably no shellfish.
- Muslim families avoid pork in any form. As with meals for Jewish children, you have to watch out for unexpected pork products in processed foods. Meat or poultry must be halal (meaning lawful), which is achieved by the method of slaughter similar to the kosher method, and then dedicated to Allah by the imam.
- Some Sikhs are vegetarian, but those who eat meat will probably avoid beef and pork. Families will want meat that has definitely not been bled in the halal or kosher method.

> **What does it mean?**
>
> **Food intolerance:** noticeable but mild negative reactions to specific foods or ingredients. There are physical symptoms, so the condition is different from simply not liking a food.
>
> **Food allergy:** more serious symptoms, such as itching, rash, nausea or vomiting, as the body reacts to the substance (see **www.allergyuk.org**).
>
> **Anaphylaxis and anaphylactic shock:** severe and life-threatening reactions such as closing-up of the throat, severe asthma, significant drop in blood pressure, shown by weakness or floppiness.

Disability and ill health

Partnership with parents is crucial, but so is a real effort by practitioners to see the world through children's eyes. Children whom adults describe as 'having special needs' do not necessarily feel 'special' in a positive way.

- Some children evade health routines that are crucial to their well being because it matters more to them to reduce their apparent difference from their peers. Children who need glasses or equipment to support their hearing sometimes 'lose' their aids on a regular basis.
- Older children and young people are sometimes resistant to taking on the necessary responsibility for their serious condition, like diabetes. The transition into older childhood and then adulthood can bring new, tough phases for families.
- Younger children may react to dismissive verbal and non-verbal communication from a practitioner who indicates, even slightly, that the child's condition demands extra time or effort. Children wish to downplay a difference that this adult is making into a troublesome problem.
- Time spent listening to children will help you to understand the troubles that can accompany disability and ill health, even when the condition seems minor to adults. Children with eczema, even mild versions, can feel very self-conscious. I did not understand this reality until my daughter explained how some children in her primary school believed eczema was a sort of contagious 'lurgy'.

Medication

No early years provision or school should impose a blunt no-medicine ground rule. Generally speaking, if children have no additional health issues, then sick children are better cared for at home and their peers (and staff) are protected from infection. However, a 'We don't give any medication' stance works in a discriminatory way, when medication or other health aids are crucial for a child's continuing well being.

The DfES issued guidance on managing medicines in school and early years provision (**www.education.gov.uk/publications/standard/publicationDetail/Page1/DFES-1448-2005**). This guidance applies to England, but raises many practical issues that are relevant across the UK. For some children, regular medication is part of normal daily life. Other children have medication that needs to be administered in an emergency. Pain-control medication may also be necessary for some children.

Scenario

At Clearwater they have worked hard in recent months to ensure shared information within and between the nursery and primary school teams. Several children who attend the nursery or school have health conditions that make them vulnerable to infection and bouts of ill health.

- Kenny, who attends the nursery, needs regular physiotherapy. With the agreement of Kenny's family, his physiotherapist undertakes one of his sessions in the nursery. Kenny is pleased for Susan and Helena to understand what he calls 'my special 'robics'. Helena has learned to undertake some of the exercises designed for Kenny.
- Winston, who has sickle cell anaemia, is more vulnerable than his friends to infections and fevers. He needs to be kept warm, especially in cold, damp weather. Susan, his key person, has found ways to protect his well being without annoying Winston, who really likes outdoor play. Winston also experiences serious bouts of illness and has to go into hospital. Susan ensures that he receives letters, photos and drawings, so that Winston knows he is being kept in mind by his friends at nursery
- Partnership with parents has helped Susan and Helena to know important personal warning signs for a child. Winston's mother took them carefully through what a sickle cell crisis looks like for Winston, and under what circumstances the nursery must call the family.
- Joanne lives with asthma and partnership started when she joined the nursery and her father explained what kind of events tended to trigger an attack for his daughter. The nursery was careful to pass everything on to Joanne's class teacher, and to the playground staff, when she moved to the primary school.

Comments

The team aim to use their knowledge to keep children safe without over protecting them. But it is sometimes hard to maintain this difficult balance.

What ways have you found to meet the needs that arise from disability or ill health and yet still ensure children have an enjoyable childhood?

Best practice is that practitioners are informed, and when necessary trained, so that they can meet disabled children's ordinary health needs and predictable emergency help, such as using an EpiPen adrenalin-injection set or an asthma inhaler.

- Keep proper written records of parents' permission and, where appropriate, a note of each administration of medicine.

- Ensure that everyone in the team has the basic information. It is risky for children when only their key person understands what should be done and when.
- You would usually keep bottles of medicine locked in a safe cupboard. However, some medication, like children's asthma inhaler or EpiPen, must travel with them, especially in a large primary school. Some children have been put at risk by uncompromising rules about locking up all medication.
- Share information in the whole team. For example, everyone must know what to do, and what not to do, when a child with epilepsy has a seizure. You can learn through partnership with parents, but can also find advice on the relevant website (in this case **www.epilepsy.org.uk**).

Some conditions are life threatening and you may experience the loss of a child who has been part of your home, or attended your nursery, school or club. Adults often have difficulty in dealing with bereavement, especially so when a baby or child has died. It is important to be honest with the children in your care; they will know something serious has happened. Children become more upset, and very confused, when adults refuse to talk about what has happened. Some distressed adults are even tempted to lie, maybe to say that a child is still in hospital or has moved away.

You need to find ways of explaining that young children can understand, but do not be tempted to gloss over facts and feelings. Avoid saying or implying that a child's death 'was for the best, she is out of her suffering now'. This 'happy release' approach does not make the child's parents feel better. The clichéd phrase can also puzzle children who know their friend had a lot of pain, but they still miss her very much, so who is happy in this situation?

If you want to find out more

You will find useful fact sheets and suggestions for information and storybooks from:
- ACT **www.act.org.uk**
- Cruse-Bereavement Care **www.crusebereavementcare.org.uk**

Scenario

The team at St Agnes Pre-school experienced the sadness of losing four-year-old Sasha, who had attended for nearly a year when she died. Michelle and her colleagues took time and care to face the situation.
- They told the other children what had happened and were ready to answer questions at that time and over the following days. A few children wanted to be reassured that disabled children do not all die and that people can be very ill and recover.
- Andrea was willing to put her sadness into words and was honest when asked by several children, saying 'Yes, I cried when I heard.' The team was careful to communicate that people show sadness in different ways.

EQUALITY AND INCLUSION IN EARLY CHILDHOOD

- Michelle decided that the situation called for a letter to go to all parents, explaining simply what had happened. The letter was supplemented by conversation if necessary.
- The practitioners were ready to talk about Sasha and more general feelings about loss as they arose from the children. They looked for low-key possibilities to support children's understanding of bereavement. But the books and puppet play that engaged some children were never used instead of conversation.
- Sasha's paintings remained on display, as did the photograph of the seaside trip when Sasha and her friends had such a good time. Sasha's mother and older brother came to talk with Michelle a few days after the funeral and were clearly pleased that important memories had not been tidied away.
- A month after Sasha's death, some of the children suggested that they could put together a special book of 'Remembering Sasha'.

Question

Discuss with colleagues or fellow students the main themes that emerge from this scenario for a caring and honest approach with children. You may like to combine discussion with following up the suggestions for finding out more on the previous page.

Dealing with words and actions

Equality practice with children comes alive through how you deal with everyday communication and a positive approach to guiding children's behaviour. Practitioners need to talk together about policy and discuss the many practical issues (see Chapter 9). Adult reflection is needed to unravel grown-up perspectives and knowledge from what children, sometimes very young, are still in the process of learning.

However, conversations between adults will only get you just so far. Practitioners need to deal with actual children and respond to events that unfold right in front of them. This chapter offers many examples with phrases that practitioners could say. Of course, these are not the only right words to use in these situations. Yet I believe that practitioners can work better from actual suggestions than a general encouragement that 'you have to say something'.

The main sections of this chapter cover:
- respect for different ways to communicate
- learning through conversation
- when words and actions hurt
- behaviour experienced as challenging.

Respect for different ways to communicate

Effective equality practice will partly be led by how you set a good example in positive communication and deal with words or actions that could undermine children's sense of self-worth.

Language and accent

Practitioners in all services for children and families need to show active respect for the language(s) that children speak and any different versions of English, including accent. Children are likely to follow the example you set through your behaviour. Experiences can also be planned in a flexible way that broadens children's horizons and build an understanding that there are languages other than their own home language.

You should step in if any children try out languages or accents in a mocking way, caricaturing speech that they do not understand. In school, children may be ridiculed for their accent, whether this arises because English is an additional language for children or because they do not speak with a local accent. If you talk and listen to the children, you may conclude that some harassment is racist and deal with the incident accordingly (see from page 136). However, early years and school practitioners should recognise that any children can be tormented over their accent. Troubles between children do not stay within neat conceptual boundaries drawn up by adults.

I have certainly known some middle-class children (White and Black) persistently harassed for having a 'posh' accent by other children in their school class (White and Black), whose social background was apparently more working class. Some tormentors were successfully hiding their social class origins by learning a different accent and way of talking, in order to gain acceptance from their preferred friendship group. Children living in England may be teased for a Welsh, Irish or Scottish accent – or not, of course. But English children, whose families have moved to other parts of the UK, have sometimes been targeted on the basis of their English accent and identity. In Scotland, for instance, some areas harbour significant anti-English prejudice.

Younger children learn the language(s) and accent present in their family home. Older children often adjust their words and way of speaking to merge with other groups. They may choose to speak in different ways with their friends and in the school playground from how they speak in the classroom or at home. In neighbourhoods with ethnic group diversity, some words and phrases cross over between groups through the children and adolescents.

Different travelling communities speak different languages (see page 57). Children from Romani Gypsy and Irish Traveller ethnic groups, and more recent arrivals to the nomadic way of life, may mostly share the English language with peers and practitioners, but some words may vary in usage. For instance, children may use the word 'bad' to mean 'ill', 'kushti' for 'good' or 'glaze' for glass. Irish Traveller children may share the more general Irish usage of the word 'bold' to cover what English children would recognise as 'naughty' or outspoken in a disrespectful way.

Take another **perspective**

Practitioners need to model respect and set a good example of courtesy that can be followed by children. The basic approach has to be 'I'm sorry, I don't understand what you're saying' or 'I don't know what that word means. Could you please explain with some other words?' This approach avoids placing responsibility unfairly with a child through 'You're not making sense' or 'Speak more clearly.'

Children learning more than one language

For many children around the world, it is completely normal to learn more than one language in early childhood. Children in fully bilingual families may learn two languages at the same time at home when they are very young. Other children

Using sign language

Children with physical disabilities, with or without additional learning disabilities, may need to communicate in ways other than words. Adults and peers have to be close and able to watch the child. Small gestures and sounds may communicate clear messages once you get to know a child. Some children may use, or be learning to use, sign language.

Within the UK deaf community, children and adults are likely to use British Sign Language (BSL) or Irish Sign Language (ISL). Young children and those with severe communication and learning disabilities are likely to be taught the Makaton sign system (see **www.makaton.org**). This approach uses speech together with a selected vocabulary from BSL and symbols. Makaton is carefully structured so that young children first learn the signs for basic needs and more complex ideas are introduced step by step.

Take another **perspective**

Appropriate guidelines for communication with disabled children build on basic courtesy and add specific understanding about the individual child. The discourtesies that can enter adult communication with all children are worsened by assumptions about disabled children. Thoughtless adults assume that children do not attend to words unless they are said directly to their face. But all children are alert. They notice the dismissive adult body language of shrugs and gestures, or behaviour that implies children are interruptible.

Scenario

The team at Crest Road Early Years Centre is careful to consider how 'special needs' work in practice. At the outset Freddy's peers were confused and annoyed with him. Nell, his key person, explained that Freddy was as big as them in size, but his thinking brain worked more like that of a younger child (Freddy's development is affected by Down's syndrome).

The other children became confident that Freddy was not going to be allowed to grab toys because he was 'special'. Several children were keen to learn sign language, known to them as 'Freddy-talk', and were soon able to understand simple requests. There were then opportunities for practitioners to say, 'Well done, you've understood Freddy wants to come into the block corner. Thanks for making space.' This approach was more effective than a general 'Please be nice to Freddy.'

Comments

It is a great advantage if at least one practitioner within a large group setting has learned to sign. In a very small team, or working on your own, you may not learn the skill until an individual child needs this attention.

Hearing children, with no disabilities affecting language development, are often enthusiastic co-learners.

Signing definitely does not mean that you stop talking – use both methods of communication.

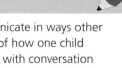

Pause for reflection

Disabled children, who have limited spoken language, often communicate in ways other than speech. If you have the opportunity, build up a written record of how one child communicates without words. Your understanding will have started with conversation with the child's parent and continued partnership. However, you will learn more as the weeks and months pass and the child will develop more ways of communicating with you or peers.

Explain to parents what you are doing and share the information you gather. You might look at any of the following aspects.

- How does Louisa use sounds, perhaps a few words, facial expression or gesture to communicate?
- How does Tom show that he likes something – food, drink, a game?
- How does Louisa show that she does not like something or wants to stop?
- What kinds of fun communication does Tom like: touch and tickling, making faces, blowing raspberries or sequence games like 'Round and round the garden'?

Talking and listening

Talk directly with disabled children and ensure that the other children and parents follow your positive model.

- Talk at a normal volume and dissuade any adult or child who raises their voice to a disabled child. Shouting does not make words any clearer. In fact, raised voices can be intimidating to a child and actually distort the words for a deaf child with partial hearing or who is trying to lip-read.
- Sometimes a child may be helped by a slower pace of communication, but not to the point where the words sound patronising. Use shorter sentences and pauses to make sure that a child has understood and to give listening space for a reply.
- You can share practical hints with children and fellow adults: 'Tell Charlotte your name. She can't see you and she hasn't got used to the sound of your voice yet.' Any explanations that you give on children's behalf should include them through your words, warm gaze or touch. Perhaps the child cannot speak for herself, because she is still very young or her disability affects her speech.
- Deal firmly, although courteously, with disrespectful comments made in front of disabled children but that ignore them. Avoid blunt criticism of a fellow adult, or a child, who asks, 'Does he understand?' or 'Will she want a drink?' Use the opportunity to model courteous behaviour with 'Andy is deaf but he understands well. Please talk directly to him so he can see your face.' Or 'I don't know if Peter would like a drink. Why don't you ask him?' When appropriate, show how to sign a question as well as say it.
- Children can tell you in different ways about the kind of help they would appreciate and which actions are not actually helpful from their point of view. It is important to listen to how children feel, and watch so they can show you. You

need to communicate questions such as 'How would you like me to help?' rather than assuming you know when a child wants help and the best kind of assistance to give.

> ### If you want to find out more

The websites of national organisations are often good sources of information.
- National Deaf Children's Society – *Deaf Friendly Nurseries and Pre-schools* and *Deaf Friendly Teaching,* **www.ndcs.org.uk**
- Practitioners are often creative in making their own visual timetables and other resources. You can also buy visual systems. Many teams use PECS, the Picture Exchange Communication System, **www.pecs.org.uk**
- The Triangle project developed the resource *How It Is: An Image Vocabulary for Feelings, Rights and Safety, Personal Care and Sexuality,* **www.triangle.org.uk/ howitis**

For general support on communication, see:
- Dickins, M. (2011) *Listening to Young Disabled Children.* Part of the *Listening as a Way of Life* series. London: National Children's Bureau, **www.earlychildhood.org.uk**
- Dickins, M., Emerson, S. and Gordon-Smith, P. (2004) *Starting with Choice: Inclusive Strategies for Consulting Young Children.* London: Save the Children Fund.

Learning through conversation

Children are intrigued by visible differences and any new experiences for them. Their comments and questions may be phrased bluntly – in comparison with how adults express themselves – but curious young children do not usually intend to be rude or discourteous.

The best way for you to react to genuine questions is with simple and honest replies. Yet adults, who deal confidently with questions about worms or the weather, often become uneasy when children's comments touch upon skin colour, visual signs of cultural background or disability.

Dealing with questions and comments

Encouraging children to develop positive attitudes goes hand in hand with a straightforward response to their questions or reaction to their comments.
- Keep your replies simple, bearing in mind the child's age. If you answer questions willingly, then children will ask you again if they want more information or are puzzled. It is best for you to pause and ask, 'Is that clear?' or 'Have you got another question?' rather than go on and on.
- Give children accurate, factual information. Sometimes, the correct answer may be along the lines of 'Some people believe that ...' rather than your saying that it is, or is not, the case.

- Ideally, answer children's questions at the time they ask, because this is when they are interested to know. On the rare occasions when you really cannot reply, make sure that you find out and get back to a child.

Figure 7.1 Conversations can arise at any time

Scenario

Consider different ways to handle this common situation. Maria is childminder to four-year-old Nick. Last week, three-year-old Satvinder joined him. This morning, Nick asked Maria in front of Satvinder and his mother, 'Is Satvinder a girl then, cos he's got plaits?'

This is a choice point for Maria.

Suppose she goes in this direction. Maria feels embarrassed and says sharply, 'Don't be so cheeky, Nick' and adds, 'Sorry' to Paranjit (Satvinder's mother), who looks uncertain about what to do but decides to say, 'That's all right.'

What is the consequence of this choice? Nick most likely did not intend to be cheeky; he asked a fair question with four-year-old social skills. He may feel criticised and avoid asking Maria similar questions in the future. Paranjit has been placed in an awkward position, as if she believes Nick intended to be rude. Satvinder feels everybody is talking about him as if he is invisible.

Pause and rewind to the choice point ...

But suppose Maria went in this direction. She might still feel embarrassed, since her relationship with Paranjit is new, but she does not allow that emotion to determine her response. When Nick asks his question, Maria replies, 'Satvinder is definitely a boy just like you. But you're right, his hair is different from yours' and Maria's glance now brings in Satvinder and Paranjit as she says, 'Maybe we could talk about why that is.' Maria has left it open for Paranjit to speak up, if she wishes. But Maria can easily offer a simple explanation that Satvinder's family is Sikh and Sikh people do not cut their hair (see page 97).

Comments

Young children are accustomed to addressing information questions to an adult. So you often need to bring in other people by words or eye contact, to avoid excluding them from the conversation.

Early in my career, I made the same mistake as Nick when talking with a day nursery colleague. She corrected my wrong assumption that a young child was a girl, without making me feel uncomfortable or foolish. Then it was easy for me to ask my colleague for more information to extend my knowledge.

Adults are responsible for dealing with their emotions so that feelings of discomfort or embarrassment do not get in the way.

- Do not dodge giving a proper answer by evasive replies such as, 'You're too young to understand' or 'We're all the same inside.'
- If you feel uneasy about the question, resolve these feelings directly. Avoid pushing your discomfort onto the child with unfair comments like 'Don't be nosy' or 'It's rude to stare.'
- Use opportunities to help young children learn genuine courtesy. Ensure that you model courteous words and actions. Unjustified accusations of rudeness muddle the situation and often annoy children because the adult comment is unfair.

Children deserve honest and straightforward replies, and some conventional replies are not helpful. Children who ask, 'Why are some people Black?' are sometimes still told it is because the child or adult has been in the sun, or came originally from a hot country. This inaccurate reply often leads to further, reasonable questions like 'Can I get very dark this summer, if I stay out in the garden?' or 'Antonio is from Spain and that's a hot country, so why isn't he really dark like Rashida?'

A more honest, and simpler, answer to a young child is that Rashida is dark because her parents are dark skinned and children generally look like their parents. An older child may be ready for the explanation that everyone's skin colour depends on how much melanin you have in your body, and that skin colour, like many other physical features, is inherited from your parents.

If you do not know the answer to a question, then say so. If at all possible, then wonder with the child, 'How could we find out?' Under some circumstances, you could suggest that a child ask another child who can answer the question. If joint research is not viable for this question, then promise that you will find out the information. Make sure that you get back to the child.

So long as you have established a good basis of partnership with parents and other family carers, it should not be a problem to start a conversation with, 'Could I please ask you about ...' and gain some reliable information about the cultural tradition or faith of this family. Of course, you have to bear in mind that there is a great deal of diversity within as well as between cultural traditions. Be careful not to assume that you can safely generalise from this family to every other family that apparently shares their faith, cultural background or country of origin.

Scenario

Sometimes, of course, children will ask you questions that relate to your own identity or personal characteristics. This conversation can help adults to tune into how children are trying to make sense of how physical differences arise.

Myfanwy comes regularly to the Falcon Square after-school club. Last week her father joined group time and taught the children some songs in Welsh. Today a small group of the younger children are busy mixing paints for some large face and body portraits. Five-year-old Lucy says to Josie (one of the club team), 'You and Myfanwy – you two have brown skin.' Josie agrees and several children, including Myfanwy, stick out arms or legs to compare skin tones. Another child says to Myfanwy, 'Your daddy, he does Welsh.' Myfanwy smiles proudly and Josie recalls the fun time with, 'Yes, John taught us some Welsh songs last week.' Lucy looks thoughtfully at Josie's arm alongside Myfanwy's and asks, 'Josie, do you do Welsh too?' Josie sees the confusion in the look as well as hears Lucy's words and replies, 'No, I can't speak Welsh. I have dark brown skin like Myfanwy because my father has that same colour skin. But my daddy grew up in Kenya. That's a country in Africa.'

Comments

Josie accepted Lucy's question as a fair attempt to work from her observation that John spoke Welsh and had a dark skin colour. But were these two characteristics linked? Josie explained simply and did not imply that Lucy was being 'silly'.

Children have gaps in their general knowledge that only become clear, and can be courteously corrected, when they feel confident to ask you questions.

Have you encountered any examples of this kind in your interactions with children?

Deal gently with words

Sometimes genuine questions may come with offhand remarks. The entire comment is not rude, but children may add words that need to be picked up in a way that leaves them able to backtrack. You will lose children's goodwill if a fair question is lost in adult criticism of single words or phrases.

Your replies can gently correct a discourteous way of asking. You can also use the chance to pass on relevant information to a child who could not be expected to have this knowledge.

- Ben looks at Rashida and asks, 'What's wrong with her?' You could answer, 'Rashida is having trouble breathing. She needs to use her inhaler.' Perhaps Ben says he will sit by Rashida 'until she feels better' and you add, 'That's thoughtful

of you, Ben. And when Rashida can breathe easier, she'd be the best person to ask about her asthma.'
- Amrita may ask, 'Why does he dribble like a baby?' You could answer, 'Joshua has difficulty swallowing, but he's not a baby. He has cerebral palsy.' You could bring Amrita alongside Joshua, if he would like her company. But you should not make Amrita feel her question is wrong by saying, 'Ssh' or 'It's not polite to look.'
- It is not helpful to say 'Joshua is just like you' when this is obviously untrue. Joshua has many interests and experiences in common with Amrita, but cerebral palsy changes his childhood in significant ways.
- Straightforward explanations are best and you need to think what image and words are likely to connect with children's current understanding. Joshua's peers may grasp something like 'The part of Joshua's brain that sends messages to his muscles doesn't work properly. That's why it's hard work for him to move where he wants.'

Blunt questions will not always come only from children; adults can sometimes be less than courteous about disability. You will promote an inclusive approach by being ready with an honest and simple explanation of what this disability or health condition means for everyday life.

The parents of disabled children can often help you with sensible explanations; they have had plenty of experience. Support organisations for a specific disability or health condition are also a good source of simple answers to questions, either from online information sheets or advice from a helpline. Many of the information books designed for children are also a good starting point for adults (see page 167). Questions can, of course, arise from disabled children themselves as well as from their peers.

Children who recycle adult comments

In early childhood, and the years of primary school, practitioners are responsible for tuning in to the world of children. Of course, you are responsible for redirecting children who use offensive terms. However, much like using swear words, children do not know at the outset that some words are less than polite or indeed seriously offensive.

Children may repeat remarks that they have heard from other people in an 'Everyone knows ...' or 'My dad says ...' mode of sharing information. The result is offensive, but a sensitive practitioner acknowledges that the child is not being directly bigoted, or intending to hurt.
- Sometimes you will make a reply like 'Yes, I know some people say that about Gypsies. But I think it is a rude thing to say.' It is worth thinking beyond 'rude' because that word is not always the best choice. Consider words like 'unfair', 'thoughtless', 'untrue', 'not true of everybody' or 'wrong', depending on the context.

- Sometimes children's view of a situation is inaccurate because they have been misinformed by an adult who struggled to handle their question. Perhaps Ben announces that Amrita is dark because 'God painted her that colour – my grandad told me.' You need to say, and include Amrita with your eyes as you speak, 'No, Amrita was born with her warm, dark skin colour. Everyone looks a lot like their parents. Skin colour has nothing to do with being painted.' Since you have contradicted a member of Ben's family, make time to explain to his mother at the end of the day.
- Children will sometimes repeat a word that is in normal usage in their family. They will therefore be puzzled about your objection and you need to acknowledge, 'I believe you that your daddy says that word. But people who use wheelchairs don't like being called that. They find it rude, so I don't want to hear you say it about Joshua.'
- Children learn the vocabulary of offence that is used by older children and adults in a neighbourhood. Young children in Northern Ireland and parts of Scotland hear, and see written in graffiti, offensive ways to refer to whether families belong to the Catholic or Protestant denomination of Christianity. Practitioners need to answer children's questions and explain what the terms mean, but should also point out that the words are a rude way to refer to faith.

Scenario

Today in Crest Road Early Years Centre Lisa and Zainub were helping Nell to lay the tables for lunch. Lisa suddenly asked, 'Why does Zainub wear that funny scarf?' Nell replied, 'I don't think Zainub's head scarf is "funny". She and her mummy wear scarves because their family follows a tradition that women and girls cover their heads.' Zainub looked up from the other table and commented that some of her peers did not cover their heads. Nell acknowledged, 'You're right. Not everyone wears a scarf like you and your mummy.' There was a short pause and Zainub said firmly, 'It's bad when you don't cover your hair.' Nell judged it was important not to let this dismissal pass – any more than with Lisa's remark. Nell replied, 'Well, Zainub, some families believe it is fine for girls and women to show their hair. People have different views on what are the proper ways of dressing.'

Children will feel confident that practitioners are even-handed because the team takes an equivalent approach to similar situations. The previous week, Nell's colleague, Jonathon, had heard Lisa telling Zainub, 'But you can't be the princess. I have to be the princess. You must have yellow hair to be a princess.' Jonathon intervened to say, 'Lisa, that's not actually true, you know. There are lots of princesses around the world who look like Zainub. What makes you say princesses must have yellow hair?'

Comments

Conversations with children might provoke you to look carefully at the information and storybooks on your shelf, as well as what you can borrow from the library.

Are children able to see positive images of different ways of dressing?

Have your storybooks implied a world in which princesses always look White European and have long blond tresses? Perhaps you need a book like *My Very First Book of Princesses* by Caitlin Matthews (published by Barefoot Books and available from **www.smilechild.co.uk**).

Reflect on what really matters to children in how adults deal with boundaries and rules about behaviour. What will help children learn and, when necessary, redirect their own behaviour?

The principle of fairness is central. Young children probably develop fairness as their first philosophical concept, although initially in the negative version of 'That's so unfair!' The following five basic points have shone out from what children have said to me over the years. These fair rules about rules are not suspended because equality issues are central to a situation.

1 Rules shouldn't be so difficult that you can't help breaking them.
2 The rules apply to everyone; there must be a very good reason to let children off any rules.
3 Adults should listen when you explain why you did something.
4 If adults want you to tell about bad stuff (rather than hit people), then they mustn't make things worse when you ask for help.
5 It's only fair that adults have to obey all the rules as well.

Logging incidents

Written policy and team discussion need to be clear about unacceptable behaviour and words that are 'not welcome here'. However, adults have to be equally clear about how they prefer children to behave and not slip into a behaviour policy that lists only what is not allowed – whether the focus is specifically on equality or not.

It has become usual that schools have to write up and investigate any incidents that are judged to be racist (which tends to include aspects of ethnic group and culture), sexist or homophobic. Young children on school grounds, in reception class, can be affected by this requirement. It is unclear in guidance whether other early years provision, with even younger children, is expected to follow suit.

Readers will need to consult the guidance issued by their local authority and understand what they are required to do. Please also explore how any guidance enables you to meet your professional obligation for best equality practice alongside sound knowledge of child development and also being just and fair. This section offers some food for thought. Please use the ideas to support discussion and clarity in your own setting.

One of the potential difficulties of common guidelines is that the main determinant of whether an incident is to be judged as racist, sexist or otherwise offensive is whether the person on the receiving end feels it to be so. This stance was aimed as a challenge to 'It's just a joke' or 'S/He called me a … first.' The balance is now more that concerned practitioners have to log first and then later consider the details of exactly what happened, intentions, motivations and relative contributions to the critical incident.

It is difficult to see how common guidelines deal with the key concept of 'necessary and sufficient'.

- It is necessary for children to differ by race or sex for anyone to contemplate the possibility that a play dispute is an example of racism or sexism. The same principle applies when one child has a disabling condition and the other does not.
- Yet natural justice would say that the fact that Oliver is Black and Linda is White is not sufficient to say that heated words between them must be explained by and attributed to racism, if either of them feels that way.

Equality legislation makes it clear that any guidelines over racist incidents should definitely include the possibility that Black children could be racist towards White children, or that children from different Black Minority Ethnic groups could insult and harass each other along racist lines. Linda is a girl and Oliver is a boy. So the same logic over sexism would direct practitioners to accept, on face value, either child's conviction that they were not allowed to play because of their sex. There could be an identical sequence of dispute between Linda and Joanna, yet neither could invoke 'It's because I'm a girl.'

We have reached this situation out of good intentions to address and challenge offensiveness and establish positive attitudes in the younger generation. Wise school, and out-of-school, teams know very well that creating a written record (and when obliged, submitting the incident log to a national government department) does not in itself create a harmonious community for children or adolescents. The problem of the current balance is that practitioners are directed to act as if an incident is reprehensible on equality grounds, and log it as such, before they have undertaken the kind of listening and talking that elicit what has happened – an exploration which children have the right to expect.

This kind of direction raises the question of how easy it is for children (or adolescents) to prove that they have not been racist, sexist or homophobic. Equally, some interpretations appear to leave very limited scope for the child on the receiving end to reject the 'victim' label and for his or her viewpoint to be accepted. Battered or harassed children definitely deserve full support. However, resilient children may take the genuine stance that 'He's my friend and neither of us should have said what we did.' It is unacceptable if this child's strong preference for moving past the temporary argument is interpreted by adults as denial of distress.

I have encountered situations like the scenario on page 129, where a remark like that made by (fictional) George had to be logged as a racist incident and a letter sent to the family. The emotional temperature soared, young children were flummoxed about what was happening and no progress was made to turn a negative family outlook towards something more acceptable.

The ideas, and differing viewpoints, raised in this section, benefit from reflection and open discussion in a team or course group. You will find examples of the two opposing views in:

- Gillborn, D. (2008) *Racism and Education: Coincidence or Conspiracy?* London: Routledge.
- Hart, A. (2009) *The Myth of Racist Kids: Anti-Racist Policy and the Regulation of School Life.* London: Manifesto Club.

What behaviour do you want to encourage?

Adults can make a difference to how children's attitudes develop. Yet you have to be realistic about how a positive outlook might work with real children in practice. Over the last few decades, the balance of discussion within anti-discriminatory practice has been much more about highlighting and stopping unacceptable actions and words. We need more reflective practice about the following questions.

- How might children with positive attitudes actually behave? How do you spot children who have really taken on board the equality message?
- In what ways do you support children towards alternative words when they are legitimately cross with someone and tempted to use the difference in group identity (sex, ethnic group, faith, disability – anything) as a verbal battering ram?

Children will not always like each other and they will choose some friends to whom they are closer than the rest of a group. Children will have disagreements and they will sometimes be rude to one another. Realistically, you cannot hope for a situation in which everybody always gets along or nobody is ever left out of the play. A more sensible goal is that children will relate to one another as individuals, so that friendships develop from shared interests. You want to create a situation in which children can focus on what they have in common, as well as acknowledging that they are not all the same. But differences are not about better or worse.

Early Years in Belfast has worked together with the Peace Initiatives Institute in Colorado, USA, to develop support materials to help children in the early years and primary schools to find common ground with children who initially appear different. The materials, including short animated stories, approach different aspects of equality and are suited for adjustment in line with local divisions between communities and sources of conflict. The key phrase spoken by children is, 'All of us are different. It's what makes us you and me.' When children experience shared concerns, their sense of natural justice can support fellow-feeling. It is not OK to hurt Erin because her family go to a different church. Nor is it all right to be nasty to Omar's daddy just because some people who look a bit like him did bad things.

The programme was evaluated by Paul Connolly in 2005 and short-term effects were promising in the sense that young children seemed to be more aware of how their peers could be excluded and were more willing to be inclusive in their play. Find out more about Media Initiative for Children on the Early Years website: **www.early-years.org/mifc/**.

Figure 7.2 Children who can play together are able to discover shared interests

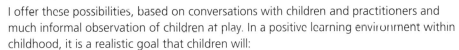

Pause for reflection

I offer these possibilities, based on conversations with children and practitioners and much informal observation of children at play. In a positive learning environment within childhood, it is a realistic goal that children will:

- make friendships and play alliances that sometimes bring together boys and girls, or children of different ethnic groups, when this opportunity is available

- sometimes be angry with each other but avoid resorting to insults based on other children's social or ethnic group, their sex or any disability

- change habits of action and language that they bring from elsewhere; so some children will actively defend a friend who has been insulted in ways that may be acceptable in their own family or social group

- learn open-mindedness about different traditions of dress, diet or language, rather than dismissing a different way as 'odd' or 'stupid'

- understand that courteous behaviour applies to everyone; it is no more acceptable for a Black African child to insult a peer with Down's syndrome than it would be for a White English child

- learn to make appropriate allowances for disabled children; but thereafter it is fair that children expect their peers to follow the ground rules for the whole group (see page 144).

What have you noticed?

What general points would you add to the list above?

Do you have some specific examples of my general points?

Compare your observations with colleagues within the same setting, in a childminding network discussion or with fellow students (ensuring that individual children cannot be identified).

Discuss whether, in your practice, you tend to focus most on unacceptable words and action. Do you notice, and acknowledge, when children behave in a fair and equitable way? What does this look and sound like?

Avoid a 'hierarchy of hurt'

During the 1990s one strand of equality practice developed that rests on a view of power that is all about adult perspectives. You may still encounter the stance that offensiveness from a Black child to a White is less important than the reverse because of the reality of discrimination and unequal power relations within UK society. I believe this stance is unacceptable because it imposes consequences on young children which are completely unrelated to what they have done. The unequal approach also disregards the serious risk of communicating to some children that their hurt matters less, for reasons over which they have no control.

This mistaken approach is sometimes described as working within a hierarchy of hurt, or of oppression. Children are far less likely to support their peers if they experience that some hurtful remarks seem to matter more to the adults. A White girl will be very hurt by a Black peer who taunts, 'You're adopted. That means your real mother didn't love you!' The child who was adopted deserves equal care and concern for her feelings as her peer should experience when on the receiving end of distressing racist remarks.

Children are far more likely to appreciate social injustice towards some of their peers when their personal concerns and hurt feelings are respected within their own social world. Children develop a strong sense of natural justice and can be very annoyed when they feel unfairly treated. They also tend to dismiss adults who impose the perceived injustice.

The hierarchy of hurt approach has tended to be linked with the belief that racism is a one-way route for bigotry, where racist behaviour is defined exclusively from White people to Black people. A similar stance over sexism claims that males cannot, by definition, be disadvantaged or offended through sexism. Such a value stance would now be at odds with equality legislation (page 21). Constructive approaches in work with adults, as well as children, seek common ground from which to move on in a positive way. For example, look at the approach of The

National Coalition Building Institute **www.ncbi.org.uk/** or The One Small Step campaign in Northern Ireland **www.onesmallstepcampaign.org/**

Scenario

The team at Falcon Square after-school club strive for good relations with all their link primary schools. They are aware that Brownstone Primary has recently overhauled its behaviour policy and brought in 'a zero-tolerance approach to racist bullying'.

Daniel and his colleagues have noticed that Myfanwy, who attends Brownstone, has been distressed at pick-up time all this week. Today Daniel sees that Myfanwy's bag is damp and sticky. With encouragement, she confides that three girls keep being 'really horrible' to her and they empty juice drinks into her bag. Daniel is close by as Myfanwy starts to tell her father at the end of the session.

The following week John, Myfanwy's father, asks to talk with Daniel about what happened at Brownstone. Yesterday he had spoken to his daughter's teacher, who said steps would definitely be taken; the school would not tolerate such behaviour. John recounts the frustrating conversation he had today with the class teacher, who was keen to reassure him that the bullying was not racist and had nothing to do with Myfanwy's skin colour. The teacher went on, 'It was just some girls being silly and calling Myfanwy "posh". I'm afraid children get that, if they live in the bigger houses round here.' John is dissatisfied with this response, feeling that the school has dismissed his daughter's distress and the deliberate damage to possessions. John asks for Daniel's reaction and advice about the next step.

Please note: this scenario is not implying that every school with this kind of policy runs a hierarchy of hurt. But some policy into practice does slide in this direction. The issues need to be raised.

Questions

1 What do you think? Is it less important, from Myfanwy's perspective, to be bullied over presumed social class than skin colour?

2 What would you suggest if you were in Daniel's position?

Name calling matters

Offensive comments and persistent name calling are a fact of life for many children. Some children are coping with physical attack, or the kind of rough treatment that their peers try to pass off as 'just having a laugh'. But this generation of children, like their parents, are more likely to be coping with the impact of persistent verbal attacks. There are times for careful ignoring of minor misbehaviour, but it is unwise to let offensiveness pass without comment. When a child is sure that you heard, your silence will be taken as acceptance, or even approval, of what was said. My cautionary remarks on page 130 about logging of incidents in no way reduces my commitment to practitioners who address problems between children in a firm and constructive way.

Studies of primary school experiences – for instance, by Cecile Wright (1992) or Barry Troyna and Richard Hatcher (1992) – have described the distress and daily grind for children when racist name calling and other verbal abuse are not effectively tackled by a school. Troyna and Hatcher also point to the importance of ensuring that White children have strong and positive sources of identity. Otherwise, children with limited sources of self-esteem are tempted to make themselves feel better by targeting minority ethnic groups. Children in this situation may well have strong adult models from their family and local neighbourhood that push them in this direction.

On the receiving end

Children can feel desperate if they are regularly hearing rude remarks about themselves or their family, for whatever reason. They need adults to deal with incidents in ways that will help the child on the receiving end of hurtful words, or behaviour, to feel better. They deserve and need the following responses:

- Comfort, through your words or friendly touch, if they wish. A child who has been very hurt by another's words may be close to tears and welcome a reassuring cuddle. I appreciate that many school teams, and unfortunately also some early years settings, have become highly anxious about touch (see page 100). But girls, and boys too, in early childhood will not believe you really care about their hurt if contact is denied when they clearly want it.
- A clear message from you that you like these individual children and feel positive about any source of identity that has been under verbal attack. Be guided by the children's feelings and what you have learned about their personal preferences.
- Reassurance that children do not have to tolerate physical ill treatment or name calling in order to be accepted by their peers. The key point about a joke or a 'bit of fun' is that everyone enjoys it, not that some children find it amusing and others are distressed.

Take another **perspective**

It is worth reflecting on the reasons why it is unacceptable for children to use certain words or behave in particular ways. Wise adults have some answers for 'Why?' since children increasingly pose that question.

- Mild, non-specific reprimands are unhelpful: 'That's not a nice thing to say' does not offer children much in the way of explanation.
- The answer on words may be that the remark was 'unfair', 'untrue', 'cruel', 'unkind' or another appropriate word. You can be guided by the expressed hurt or outrage of the child on the receiving end.
- The answer about actions will need to connect with ground rules about how 'we all behave in our nursery/school/club' or, for childminders, 'what happens here in my home when we have a disagreement'.

You and your colleagues need to talk together and decide a consistent approach that will be applied when you do not have time to think. There must be consistency within a team. Children feel frustrated, even abandoned, by adults when behaviour policy is implemented fitfully and some adults do not respond appropriately when children do as they are asked and 'tell' rather than lash out with fists and feet.

However, all practitioners need to be kind to themselves. Sometimes realisation comes after the event: 'I wish I'd said that' or 'That was foolish, I shouldn't have reacted that way.' Avoid wasting energy on regret, and focus on how you will behave differently faced with a similar situation in the future.

Children who give it out

Your approach to children who have given hurt or offence needs to be consistent with a positive approach to guiding behaviour.

- Explain why a remark is unacceptable rather than trying to make children feel guilty with 'Don't you think that was an offensive (or racist) thing to say?' Is there any way to answer this pseudo-question in a way that will satisfy an irritated adult? Honest adults need to say, if necessary, 'I find that phrase offensive because …'.
- Children's attitudes are in the process of forming and you have a chance to influence them. It is unacceptable adult behaviour to use sweeping labels for a young child like 'racist' or 'sexist', any more than you should label them as 'lazy' or 'spiteful'. Negative labels leave a child with no space to listen and to find another way of reacting.
- Furthermore, a bad adult habit of dismissing children through labelling can be recycled by children against each other. I have encountered the results of misguided equality practice with primary and secondary pupils who have learned to attack any behaviour that annoys them by shouting at their peers 'That's racist!' or 'You're sexist!'
- Dislike the behaviour; but show you continue to like and accept the child as a person. So you say to Sally, 'I think that was a rude name to call Isaac' rather than 'You are such a rude girl!' You might judge that it is an appropriate time to say a bit more: perhaps 'Yes, it is true that Isaac and his family are Jewish. But it is not OK that you use that to insult him.'

Scenario

The team in Clearwater nursery class used to tell children to think about the feelings of another child. But they realised that they lost the children by trying to get them to be empathetic on the spot.

Today Alice has verbally lashed out at Simon with 'You're rubbish! All boys are completely thick. My mum says men are a waste of space.' In the past, Helena would have tried something along the lines of 'You've made Simon really upset. He feels as bad as you would if he had been that nasty to you. How do you think you would feel if Simon said you were rubbish?' Helena has joined the nursery from time spent with seven-year-olds. She noticed that, even in middle childhood, many children still do not connect with this emotional maze, especially when feelings are running high.

So instead, Helena says, 'No, Alice, it's not OK to tell Simon he is "rubbish" and words like that.' Alice looks attentive, so Helena judges she can add, 'I wouldn't let him trash you because you're a girl, and you don't trash Simon just because he's a boy.' Helena has

Comments

Some children and their families have to deal with unacceptable behaviour from members of another ethnic group. It is still important that you do not ignore negative generalisations dismissing entire groups because of the bad behaviour of some individuals.

Scenario

Early years, school and out-of-school practitioners cannot step aside from rejecting attitudes when they emerge right in front of them through children's language or play. However, your response needs to be holistic.

At Crest Road Early Years Centre the team wanted to develop a consistent response, as hard as they found some of the situations. Darren was ready to step in with words when Beverley tried to repeat her family's view with, 'Them Mosems are very bad. They blow people up!' Darren commented kindly but firmly, 'Are you talking about people who are Muslims, Beverley? That's an awful lot of people to call "bad". It's not true that everyone who is a Muslim wants to hurt people.'

But two weeks later Jonathon knew it was equally important to acknowledge Amir's excited call as he bashed over his building with a truck, 'Hurray! Boom! They all deaded now!' Jonathon sat down close to the play and said, 'Amir, I feel sad about people who are killed – not glad about it.' Amir looked puzzled, 'But it's good to kill bad people.' Jonathon continued, 'Yes, I know people are killed in wars. But I don't think it's a time to say "Hurray".'

The centre team is well aware that Beverley's family express bigoted views about local Muslim families, but it is just as relevant that Amir's father has expressed open approval of recent terrorist bomb incidents.

Comments

These situations are not at all easy. But teams and individual practitioners such as childminders need to take an even-handed approach to bigotry and rejection by any family of another faith or ethnic group.

Have you faced a similar situation? What was your response? Would you take a different approach now?

In Northern Ireland, more than one generation of children grew up through times of violence and divisive social conflict. Equality initiatives in this part of the UK are well grounded in anti-sectarianism, in addition to other aspects of equality practice. However, supportive work with all types of practitioners has needed to acknowledge that these adults are also affected by the social stresses. It is that much harder to support young children if adults never get the opportunity to deal with what recent history has done to them.

Led by Rosie Burrows and Brid Keenan, *We'll Never be the Same Again* (2004) is the report of a Barnardo's project in Northern Ireland that arose from the pilot work in *Parenting in a Divided Society*. The materials extend to support for practitioners who work with children. The main project focused on parents but has strong messages for practitioners who cope with stressful conditions partly by hoping that children are unaware (**www.barnardos.org.uk**).

Events through the early 21st century have stirred anti-Muslim feeling (sometimes called Islamophobia) through an unjustified generalisation from some groups within Islam to everyone within the faith. Some useful materials have emerged to support practitioners, although it is rare for writers based in England to create links with the anti-sectarianism expertise from Northern Ireland.

If you want to find out more

- Adams, S. and Moyles, J. (2005) *Images of Violence: Responding to Children's Representations of the Violence They See.* Husbands Bosworth: Featherstone Education.
- Community Relations Council of Northern Ireland. **www.community-relations.org.uk**
- Connolly, P., Smith, A. and Kelly, B. (2002) *Too Young to Notice: the Cultural and Political Awareness of 3–6 Year Olds in Northern Ireland.* Belfast: Community Relations Council.
- Lane, J. and Baig, R. (2003) *Building Bridges for Our future: The Way Forward through Times of Terror and War.* Wallasey: Early Years Equality.
- Learning and Teaching Scotland has examples to explain anti-sectarianism – **www.ltscotland.org.uk/supportinglearners/positivelearningenvironments/inclusionandequality/challengingsectarianism/**
- Northern Ireland Council for Integrated Education (NICIE), *The Anti-Bias Curriculum,* **www.nicie.org.uk**

Children from refugee and asylum-seeking families

Children and their families will often need support, although this will depend a great deal on the circumstances under which they have left their country of origin. Disorientated and distressed children will not benefit from joining busy early years settings where practitioners are already overstretched. I have encountered some groups where there is insufficient personal attention for young children whose lives are relatively stable. It does not work to place children from refugee or asylum-seeker families in such settings in the vague hope that an early educational setting must be 'a good thing'. Children react to the uncertainty through their actions and there is then a high risk that 'cries for help' are treated as behaviour problems.

Any early years provision supporting refugee children and their families needs to have access to specialist advice to supplement the support you offer through daily routines and experiences. You need to be aware of the following factors.

- Children's experience may make them very vulnerable to what seem like overreactions to relatively ordinary situations. Some children may be very easily distressed or may hit out in self-protection. You need to offer emotional support and understanding, as well as guide children towards more appropriate reactions now they are in a safe place.

- Like their peers, refugee children are likely to play out their experiences: with dolls and small-world figures, through pretend play themes and in drawings or stories. Bear in mind that what you assume to be violent fantasy play, and perhaps wish to discourage, could be a literal reworking of what this child has seen. The play may be therapeutic, although you will have to guide children in order to reduce any negative impact on peers.
- Some children may wish to talk about their memories or continuing worries and some may have realistic fears for family or close friends left behind in a war zone or in refugee camps.

See page 146 for useful resources.

Assumptions combining gender and ethnic group

Gender stereotypes can shape how practitioners react to boys and girls, leading to positive or negative interpretations of children's actions and play choices (see page 40). An even-handed approach to boys seems to be further put at risk by how some practitioners relate to boys from families of African-Caribbean origin.

Cecile Wright (1992) noted that African-Caribbean boys were among the most criticised and reprimanded in the mixed classrooms she observed. The boys were told off for the kind of behaviour that was often ignored for White children. The Black boys were more prominent in school discipline procedures such as being sent out of the classroom and exclusions. Wright's observations are supported by national statistics on school exclusion. Later problems seem to have roots in boys' early school and pre-school experiences.

- Some practitioners have stereotypical beliefs that all African-Caribbean families use harsh, physical discipline. A linked belief is that the boys will find it hard to settle in out-of-home settings. This attitude can lead practitioners to treat the boys differently: they 'just' need to run around outdoors. This assumption is especially negative when early years teams fail to value outdoor learning.
- There are broad cultural differences in the use of spoken language and body language. The communication style of some African-Caribbean families can be very forthright. Boys especially may be judged by practitioners to be 'cheeky' or 'disruptive'. The usual dangers of labelling a child follow, and boys start a career as a 'troublemaker'.
- Negative judgements may be shared among a team who have not established an effective and professional policy on behaviour. Individual children have fewer and fewer options. Adults become more fearful of losing a power struggle with the boys than tackling behaviour in a positive way, including reflection on their own actions and words.

All boys need early years experience that develops positive attitudes towards learning and the school experience. Older boys and adolescents, from all ethnic group backgrounds, sometimes confide in 'safe' adults how they cultivate a tough exterior to hide an interest in study or books. Boys from an African-Caribbean background seem especially needful of positive male role models. They encounter many messages, not least from some aspects of street culture, that lead them away from valuing what they can gain from a learning environment such as school.

Figure 7.3 Children need familiar adults as a play and conversational partner

Behaviour that is 'normal' for children

Children learn patterns of behaviour from their families and any home will reflect the social and cultural identity of parents. Practitioners need to be aware of, and ready to learn more about, broad differences in behaviour and body language. Two examples follow, in which I suggest that the way to resolve the situation is different although still communicates respect.

Eye contact

A broadly western European cultural tradition is to encourage children to make eye contact with adults. Reduced or fleeting eye contact is often interpreted as inattention or shiftiness, and possible evidence of guilt. However, children whose family origins are from many other parts of the world are taught that it is courteous to drop their eyes when talking with adults, especially if being reprimanded.

In this situation I think the responsibility of practitioners is to flex to the comfort of children. You may find it hard to believe a child is listening to you when they have limited eye contact. Resolve your feelings by asking them to use words to indicate understanding, rather than requiring that they look directly at you. You are the grown-up; it is fair that you make the adjustment.

Spitting

Generally speaking, in Europe it is not accepted behaviour that children or adults spit in the street or at other people. Spitting is more acceptable in some cultures.

Spitting on the hand, or pretending to spit, is sometimes an action judged to ward off bad luck – a tradition in parts of Greece, but also a superstition for some people whose European origin is the UK. I have encountered several instances when children used spitting towards someone else to emphasise their position in an argument. Practitioners realised that the behaviour arose from the family's cultural tradition.

In this situation, I think the responsibility of practitioners is to communicate courteously to families and children, 'We have no spitting in nursery/school'. Further explanation can follow: 'I understand you think it is all right to spit. It is your choice what you do in your family. But many children here are upset and cross about this behaviour. We will help your children to make their point strongly with words.'

Disability and behaviour

A basis for non-discriminatory treatment is that fair and reasonable adjustments are made for behaviour that is a consequence of a child's condition. Thereafter, however, it is important that disabled children are expected to follow the same ground rules as their peers. If disabled children are seen to be 'allowed to get away with things', then their potential play companions will get annoyed.

Scenario

Disabled children are still boys and girls who need firm but fair adult guidance over their behaviour.

- In Clearwater nursery class, the children understand that Kenny needs space for his wheelchair. Occasionally he misjudges a turn and has collided with their constructions. Today the children in the block corner are adamant that Kenny crashed into them on purpose – not least because he reversed for another go. They want to see Helena deal fairly with Kenny.
- Ciara can be very ill as the result of coping with cystic fibrosis, but her parents have been clear in discussions with Maria, her childminder, that they want their daughter to have a playful childhood and to make friends. So they ask Maria to use the same ground rules for Ciara's behaviour that apply for Nick and Satvinder.

Comments

Some families do not find the balance expressed by Ciara's parents. Some parents, or other family members, feel so saddened by a child's disability that they struggle to set and hold to boundaries suitable for any child. Supportive practitioners can be of immense help and can offer advice without the implication that parents are 'overprotective'.

Of course, it is appropriate that parents and practitioners take account of the impact of a child's disability or health condition. Children's peers can be genuinely understanding that 'Ciara sometimes feels rotten, and that's not her fault,' or that 'Kenny sometimes makes a mistake steering his wheelchair.'

Some children live with conditions that provoke intermittent or continuous pain. Readers who experience bouts of back trouble or migraine will understand how wearing it is to cope with pain. The situation can lead even stoic adults to be cranky. There is good reason to suppose that being in constant pain may be an underlying cause of challenging behaviour from some disabled children or young people (see page 87).

Disability campaigners express concern that different kinds of settings, like schools, have been more responsive initially around equalising opportunities arising from physical and learning disabilities. However, disability also requires practitioners to recognise issues around behaviour. For example, children with autistic spectrum disorder and Asperger's syndrome can experience severe struggles to manage the details of group life in a nursery and increasingly the more formal context of school. Partnership with parents, as well as getting to know children as individuals, will help to avoid a situation in which children are unfairly held responsible for behaviour that they cannot control, without a great deal of step-by-step support.

Physical intervention and careful, safe restraint can become an issue over the behaviour of any children, but is probably heightened if children have emotional and behavioural difficulties. Part of good care in early years, school and out-of-school services has to be that adults use their greater strength wisely to keep children safe. Refusal to use touch could well be seen as neglect, a failure in the duty of care by responsible adults. Practitioners need to use close physical contact when children are plunging into an unsafe situation, or because they are hurting each other and will not stop unless an adult intervenes.

Adults should use their physical abilities with care, when action has to be prompt; this care is for the well being of the adults as well as the children. Children who are older are also usually larger. Practitioners need special training in safe physical handling, especially when children's disabilities mean that their behaviour may be unpredictable and challenging.

If you want to find out more

- Connolly, P. (1998) *Racism, Gender Identities and Young Children: Social Relations in a Multi-Ethnic Inner-City School.* London: Routledge.
- Dickins, M. (2011) *Listening to Young Disabled Children* and Road, N. (2011) *Are Equalities an Issue: Finding Out What Young Children Think.* London: National Children's Bureau, **www.earlychildhood.org.uk** (accessed 31 July 2011).
- Drifte, C. (2004) *Encouraging Positive Behaviour in the Early Years: A Practical Guide.* London: Paul Chapman Publishing. (Especially relevant for supporting disabled children.)
- High/Scope UK – DVDs and books about teaching children skills of conflict resolution, **www.high-scope.org.uk** (accessed 31 July 2011).
- Kidscape – positive approaches to behaviour and bullying, **www.kidscape.org.uk** (accessed 31 July 2011).

developmentally grounded in themselves and their familiar social world. Three- and four-year-olds still need to 'start with me'. Nothing is gained, and much can be lost, by trying to speed up children's general knowledge over equality issues.

Who can I see?

Visual images, books and play resources should be a rich source of positive images in which children can see themselves and their families. But all children also need positive messages about children, and adults, who do not look immediately familiar. Displays of all different kinds, including your book resources, are a way to offer accurate images of children and families who are not represented locally, or who are in the minority. Balance in illustrations is just as important for babies and toddlers, who have not yet worked out the representational meaning of pictures – babies are busy looking and toddlers will soon notice details – but their families will be coming regularly to your setting or own family home. Images are a form of communication between adults as well as for the children.

You can create displays through photos of shared experiences enjoyed by children who are currently in your setting or family home. Appropriate photos can be cut out of magazines and catalogues, but you can also find and print images from the internet by using a facility like searching in Google by 'Images'. Many of the organisations listed on pages 175–6 sell good-quality visual materials and illustrated books.

- Look in detail at the early years guidance for your own area of the UK and remind yourself of what is actually written around equality issues.
- Take the opportunity to look through at least one set of guidance from another part of the UK. What can you see in common with the materials with which you are most familiar? See page 28 for how to access the documents.

Figure 8.1 Any policy has to make sense for the world of young children

A question of balance

You need to consider the balance of images you offer and be aware of what else children are likely to encounter during their time with you.

- Charity catalogues, like those from UNICEF or Oxfam, sell posters and photo cards. Yearly diaries sometimes include good-quality pictures of children and families from around the world, including European locations.
- Be cautious, though, about charity posters whose target is fundraising and therefore emphasise problems and distress. If you are not careful, you can give a negative image of some parts of the world. Similar problems can arise over images of disabled and sick children. You would not extend children's knowledge about animals only from RSPCA charity appeals.

- Travel brochures can be a good source of pictures of many different countries. *National Geographic* magazine has stunning photographs, and back copies often end up in second-hand book shops.
- These images need to be balanced with more everyday images of families shopping, at mealtimes or children at school. Children need to understand countries and cultures less familiar to them through shared experiences as much as the possible differences.
- Are the children in any photos or posters from less-familiar places showing a variety of emotions: happy, excited, serious but sometimes needing comfort or looking thoughtful?
- The same question applies for images of disabled children or adults, who in real life are not permanently smiling. People with a disability sometimes feel serious, sad or fed up, not necessarily because of the disability. When children have limited contact with disabled peers, then illustrations, and books, will be the main source of their views.

Pause for reflection

It is also important to reflect on the gender balance of visual materials.

- In your setting, or home if you are a childminder, what range of pictures or photographs are obvious to children? What messages do these illustrations give to children or parents?
- Can they see caring men with young children as well as women? And are these ordinary-looking men – not all models or celebrity fathers?

You can create unique visual material by using photographs taken within your daily practice. These images can be especially effective when they are part of a learning story created with children themselves. Photos and scribing by you, and emergent or actual writing by children, build into a book about a continuing experience, such as 'How we found out about what police officers do'.

The Fatherhood Institute has a wide range of positive images of men as fathers (**www.fatherhoodinstitute.org/**).

Can I move around easily?

All public buildings now have to make reasonable modifications to ease access by wheelchair, or for anyone with a disability affecting mobility. Improvements for disabled people are usually inclusive and improve facilities for many people. For instance, sloped entrances, rather than steps, and more spacious toilets are an immense help to every adult pushing a buggy. Contact with disabled children or parents can make you reassess ease of access to, and movement around, your setting.

- Perhaps you take a considered look at how Joshua, with cerebral palsy, will move around the room. It may dawn on you that creating more space for Joshua will encourage you to remove some of the clutter that is unhelpful for the existing group. Perhaps the narrow access to your book corner is the source of avoidable, minor collisions between children.

- Andy, who is deaf, may show unease at a visually over-busy nursery. Lack of clear areas means that children cross his line of vision without warning and disrupt his play. Charlotte, who is blind, may show that you need to consider predictable routes between indoors and outdoors. However, the changes also improve the learning environment for these children's peers.

If you want to find out more

- Community Playthings has materials online about planning a child-friendly environment, for example: *Spaces* and *Creating Places*, **www. communityplaythings.co.uk**

Inclusive play resources

Early years practitioners sometimes believe that disabled children will need expensive, specialist play equipment. Some additional play resources may be useful, but many of your materials will be suitable for disabled children. Nevertheless, many items marketed for special needs are truly inclusive. All children want to enjoy the large sound-making boards, big foam wedges and ball pools. Sensory areas or rooms are often developed with disabled children in mind, but the experience is suitable for everyone.

Scenario

Michael has cerebral palsy, but that does not stop him wanting to get stuck into the sand and water play at Crest Road Early Years Centre. His parents chose Crest Road after a short, unhappy experience in another nursery where staff acted as if Michael would only be able to use 'special' equipment. Michael had also felt insulted because one practitioner in his previous setting had given him 'baby toys', apparently on the grounds that they were easier for him to handle. Some practical reorganisation was needed at Crest Road to ensure Michael could get access for his standing frame. He is fully confident now to announce 'I need my parking space!' if his peers have not left enough room.

Freddy has learning disabilities associated with Down's syndrome. Staff have to be aware that, long after his peers were ready to have play materials with very small parts, Freddy still sucks on little items. He has benefited from a range of resources at a similar developmental level. Freddy needs to practise his skills, but would soon become bored with the same play items.

Questions

1 Consider what changes might be necessary in your setting or family home as a childminder, if you were joined by a child like Michael, with mobility affected by cerebral palsy. Look for ideas on **www.scope.org.uk**

2 Reflect on what range of play materials could be of interest to Freddy, allowing for the fact that he is four years old but behaves and thinks much more like a two-year-old. Look for ideas on **www.downs-syndrome.org.uk**

team members (see also page 189). The school playground can be a lonely place for any child if adults do not take care.

Barriers that block access for disabled children are often not physical; attitudes and anxiety can get in the way. You may be aware of the extra help needed by children whose physical disability makes them wobble or whose learning disability means they cannot judge risk as effectively as their peers. Disabled children may need kind guidance (just like their peers) and will benefit from sensible adjustment of their playing space or equipment. But then children just want to get on with their play and grow in competence like their peers. Children want to have some adventures and will accept some bumps or bruises. Disabled children are not helped by excessive protection, however well intentioned.

Scenario

The team at St Agnes have reflected on possible assumptions about girls and boys as part of their effort to make better use of the outdoor space and new clambering possibilities. Here are some recent examples raised in team meetings.

- Three-year-old Angela is uncertain and today said, 'I can't go up there. My mum says girls are no good at climbing. I'll fall and hurt myself.' Andrea avoided saying bluntly that Angela or her mother were wrong. She replied, 'Well, I've known a lot of girls who are really good climbers. You could try climbing just as far as you're comfortable with. I'll be standing right here.'
- Some of the boys in the pre-school were confident with the new hockey set. But some boys, Jed and Ricky in particular, were anxious about being hit by a ball or stick. Staff acknowledged the boys' concern, and let them handle the soft balls and watch the play before opting to join in. A clear rule was also made that hockey sticks were to be lifted no higher than waist level.

The pre-school had supplemented its limited store of simple games equipment. The team has used the opportunity of Tim's work-placement period with them to show adults crossing possible gender boundaries. Andrea often leads the hockey game and soft football. Tim has been enthusiastic to learn skipping rope skills.

Questions

1 Many practitioners hold unchecked assumptions about girls and boys in play. Ideas have probably been established within your own childhood.

2 Reflect on whether you tend to wait longer with boys on a climbing frame to say, 'Isn't that a bit high?' Or do you assume girls will be more concerned about getting grubby outdoors? Do boys who are uneasy get less support or a surprised adult expression?

If you want to find out more

- Barbarash, L. (1997) *Multicultural Games.* Champaign, IL: Human Kinetics.
- Dunn, O. (2001) *Acker Backa Boo! Games to Say and Play from Around the World.* London: Frances Lincoln.
- Kidsactive. **www.kids.org.uk** – details about the National Inclusive Play Network and the Playwork Inclusion Project (PIP) (accessed 31 July 2011).

- Lear, R. (1996) *Play Helps: Toys and Activities for Children with Special Needs.* Oxford: Butterworth-Heinemann.
- Lindon, J. (2011) *Too Safe for their Own Good? Helping Children Learn about Risk and Life Skills.* London: National Children's Bureau.
- Marl, K. (1996) *The Accessible Games Book.* London: Jessica Kingsley.
- Positive Press – books about enjoyable school playtimes and games to play with children, **www.circle-time.co.uk**

Experiences for creativity

A well-rounded week for children in early years, school and out-of-school facilities should offer a wide range of resources that can extend their creative skills and interests. Some of these experiences can be genuinely self-chosen by children because you have organised a well-resourced box, corner or workshop area. Some enjoyable activities will be adult initiated, in that you have pre-planned to an extent, but then genuinely creative experiences of any kind have considerable scope for choices and decisions to be made by the children.

Music, songs and dance

Music and dance offer many possibilities and you can guide children to try a wide range. Notice who joins in and who stands on the sidelines. You could also watch out for unnecessary patterns such as the boys usually playing the noisier instruments like drums and the girls taking the triangles or tambourines.

Children enjoy songs and rhymes, with or without hand movements. Awareness of sound and sound patterns is helped by participation in a group, or when an individual child enjoys standing up to deliver a chosen song or rhyme. Ensure that the children's repertoire includes songs from different cultural traditions, starting with those represented in the group and local neighbourhood. You may be fortunate in having parents who could sing for children in languages additional to English. CDs are also available that can supplement live singing sessions. CDs are often sold with written songbooks and short explanatory leaflets giving the background to the songs.

Most musical traditions have at least some simple instruments that can be used by even young children. You can choose from a wide range of small drums, single-stringed instruments, flutes and simple whistles, xylophones, many different kinds of shakers, bells that may be shaken or small sets of bells (like gungroos) that are worn on the wrists or ankles and make music as children dance, cymbals and tambourines. See, for instance, the possibilities on offer from Music Education Supplies (**www.mesdirect.com/**).

Musical activities need to be presented positively.
- Children enjoy learning to use sound makers in particular rhythms – for instance, light Caribbean calypso rhythms or the steady thump of a British marching band.

Tim's comments led Andrea to lay out a world map in a team meeting. The visual impact led to rethinking the details of planned experiences for the children. Many of the resources were good quality but needed to be grounded in the same way that the practitioners would have done for something vaguely 'European'. Michelle made a note to call and get more appropriate detail about the 'African drummer' whom they had booked to visit.

Comments

Do you check your assumptions and general knowledge? Have you looked at a map recently? Europe is one of the smallest continents; Australia is the smallest.

Africa, Asia and South America are all substantial and include many different countries, with human variety in language, ethnic group and faith. The landscapes are also very diverse – for example, Africa is not all 'jungle', South America is not all 'Amazonian rainforest'.

Be ready to reflect on planned experiences for children that are from parts of the world less familiar to you. Some well-intentioned topics on 'Africa' are the equivalent of doing 'Europe' by dressing in clogs as a Dutch girl, tasting some baklava and dancing the Flamenco – all to a visual backdrop of the Scottish Highlands.

Pretend play

Most young children start to show imagination in their play some time in their toddler year. Their first pretend actions are fleeting but their power of imagination grows until three- and four-year-olds are able to sustain lengthy imaginative sequences, and they often return to self-chosen themes with friends over and over again. The supportive adult role is to provide flexible resources and space for play to spread out, and to be willing to be drawn in as a playful adult, who does not then take over the play.

The home corner

Children's play will reflect their experience to date, much of it from their family life. So it is important to show respect for their views, even when you do not agree with them. For instance, a group of girls may be pretend cooking and two boys are sitting waiting to be served. Carline's explanation that 'men can't cook' might be met with, 'Some men can't cook but I know a lot who can. How about next time Benjie does the cooking and you fix the wheels on the buggy?'

Some children will come from families where both sexes feel strongly that cooking is women's work, and possibly less to be respected for that reason. It is the choice of a family what they do in their own kitchen or dining area, but you can gently shift possibilities in your nursery, club or your own home as a childminder. You may be able to help this process if you become involved in the pretend play. Perhaps you respond to Benjie's peremptory, 'Tea, now!' with a firm but kindly, 'Well, who made you big king? Tell you what, I'll make you a nice pot of tea and then you can make me a cheese sandwich.'

Children will use the home corner to explore and play out everyday events and relationships. It is not the only focus of their pretend play, but can be a rich source of ideas and props. It is possible to obtain child-sized cooking equipment and different utensils that reflect different styles of cooking and eating. As well as pots and pans, you can have bowls, woks, ladles, large chopsticks or a steaming basket.

Figure 8.2 Pretend play will reflect children's own home experiences

Take another **perspective**

This area of play and learning is one in which adults have to be wary of their own assumptions.

- For instance, many UK families have a kettle in the kitchen, but in many other European countries people boil water in a small saucepan.

- Colleagues whose country of origin is within Asia may assume everyone makes tea in a saucepan and might be puzzled by a teapot.

- In various parts of the Mediterranean, or countries in northern Africa, proper coffee is made in a small heat-proof container and not with granules or powder.

- If you are unfamiliar with any cooking implements, then you need to check how they are used. You may be able to ask colleagues or parents. Suppliers may include a leaflet, or the pictures in the catalogue can help.

perhaps acknowledge that Somali or Italian children could find English amusing at the first time of hearing.

You could alert children to different written forms of language. Some bilingual families may be able to help you in displays of languages that use different alphabets and forms of writing. In school, you may be fortunate that some children can actually demonstrate writing in their home language. You can buy multilingual 'Welcome' notices. However, ideally, it would be worth developing one of your own, which draws on the languages spoken or understood by the families who actually attend your setting.

Storytelling

Storytelling can be an enjoyable supplement to reading storybooks. Many cultures around the world had, or retain, strong traditions of oral storytelling. You may be fortunate to have someone local who is a skilled storyteller. But you can become an engaging storyteller using books that you know by heart and simple props. You need to develop your skills by drawing from a range of cultural traditions represented by the stories. If at all possible, offer some storytelling supplemented with signing.

Children are often keen to become involved directly in the storytelling. Helen Bromley (2002) describes how she first came to her creative idea for story boxes. In her reception class she had a group of boys who did not seem to be engaged by books or telling stories. Then one day she made available a number of shoeboxes and flexible materials, including some animal figures. She listened, watched and realised that all the boys had many ideas for stories, and the plotlines and characters were emerging round materials that they could get their hands on.

Storytelling to support empathy

It is possible to build on children's power of imagination through storytelling as well as story reading. You can use puppets and special dolls that take on a consistent character and personal history. The overall aim of any of these approaches for equality is twofold:

1 To support children towards empathy – a sense of fellow-feeling for others and a willingness to consider how someone may feel; empathy is about finding common ground as well as grasping differences of perspective and priority.

2 To extend children's knowledge and understanding beyond their personal experience and immediate neighbourhood.

It will be important that no child feels that a story or puppet play is directly linked with a recent altercation between individual children. The aim must be to support and certainly not that children are being criticised yet again for an incident that was supposed to be finished. It is also unrealistic to expect that under-threes, and many three-year-olds, will have the conceptual understanding to link a doll's story with ideas about fair treatment of others.

Figure 8.3 Dolls and buggies are for everyone

Persona Dolls are one example of harnessing children's ability to enter a world of pretend. Babette Brown (2008) has been active in bringing the idea of Persona Dolls to the UK. These special dolls, which are given names and personal histories, can be used in a gentle way with children to help them explore the perspectives of people who appear different from themselves. These dolls, and similar resources, have the potential to support positive attitudes on any aspect of difference and are often introduced within a regular, short circle time. However, practitioners need to reflect on the balance of any story that is woven around a doll or puppet. You may wish to alert children to sources of social inequality and unfairness, but it will be unhelpful if the story evokes more pity than fellow-feeling.

Like any experiences offered to children, these resources cannot work alone; they can only complement a backdrop of daily experiences around conversation and how adults deal with behaviour (Chapter 7). There is little point in practitioners recounting a story with the alleged aim of promoting understanding of physical disability, if nobody deals with Leanna's daily experiences of being rejected for play 'because she keeps dropping things'. In fact, Leanna may feel even worse because she has noticed the inconsistency in what adults say and do. Children are

Figure 9.1 Colleagues share what they have learned from time with individual children

Scenario

Michelle, the leader of St Agnes Pre-school, has been relieved to see the back of Sophie, a practitioner who left of her own accord last term. Sophie was noticeably friendlier to parents who attended St Agnes Church, where she herself worshipped. Sophie's biased approach to partnership would be unacceptable in any case, but additionally the pre-school only rents the hall from the church council; the setting is not affiliated with the church.

Michelle had worked hard to address Sophie's unprofessional behaviour, through supervision and clear goal setting for change, but the next step would have been formal disciplinary procedures. Sophie had been offhand about activities during the exploration of Divali. She also insisted on saying a very Christian style of grace at snack time, despite a clear policy that any form of appreciation had to be more inclusive.

Sophie's words and actions had hurt Jamal's grandmother, who was the first person to raise the matter tentatively with Michelle. Ricky's father had been clearly annoyed that Sophie 'has been trying to brainwash my son' and asked that Sophie no longer be Ricky's key person. Even those parents who were favoured by Sophie's smiles and friendlier conversation looked uncomfortable about the unequal treatment.

Michelle was aware that it was increasingly difficult for parents to separate Sophie as an individual from her role as a team member. Ricky's father had summed it up: 'Michelle, I know you don't agree with how Sophie behaves, but she works in your pre-school. If you don't sort her out, it looks like you don't care about her disrespect to some of us.'

1 St Agnes Pre-school has to have a consistent approach on equality across the team, as with any practice issue. What were the main problems with Sophie's behaviour? Why was it unacceptable?

2 If Sophie had not left voluntarily, what would have been appropriate next steps for Michelle?

3 Suppose that Michelle receives a request for a job reference for Sophie. How should she communicate her serious reservations about her former colleague?

Shared values and priorities

Individuals can work together as a team, or a pair, when they are enthusiastic about what they are doing and feel that the work matters. With a shared commitment to values and an understanding of priorities, individuals can pull in the same direction. Good and effective equality practice, like any other aspects of your work, depends on a continuing experience of trust in your colleagues. Trust over equality is created from experience that colleagues are:

- reliable – they follow the pattern that has been agreed in response to children's questions and comments; they do not assume words are intentionally offensive without good cause
- consistent – they offer the same standard of courtesy to parents, and kind attention to children's personal care needs, regardless of how they may feel today, or whether their relationship with that family or child is, overall, 'easy' or 'more difficult'
- honest – they express openly in the team any doubts or uncertainties about policy and implementation; they admit if they do not know something and are ready to check out assumptions.

Taking a constructive approach

Staff teams, or groups like childminding networks, need a constructive approach to discussion and disagreement. Senior practitioners, team leaders and group facilitators need to encourage colleagues and network members to consider unchecked assumptions and reflect on their use of language. However, this interaction must be supportive, so practitioners feel they have the chance to save face and make an alternative choice. Highlighting only the 'wrong' words or expressed views can seriously undermine morale within a team or any sense of group support. A serious negative consequence is that practitioners then become much more concerned with 'what we're not allowed to say' than with considering the views that underlie the words.

It is not feasible to ignore conflict over equality; issues need to be resolved by bringing the sources of dispute or misunderstanding out into the open. Doubts and disagreements about equality practice, just like any other aspect of the work, do not go away. They bubble under the surface; some practitioners will feel resentful, some may feel disrespected, and those emotions will affect their daily practice in one way or another.

It is important to tackle under-representation so that a team, or the local service as a whole, is a more accurate reflection of society. But then each member of staff or practitioner in a local service needs to feel properly included and not pushed into being a full-time representative of a grouping that is only part of their individuality. A disabled colleague will have opinions about many issues, not only disability. A male practitioner should not forever have to give the 'man's point of view'.

If you want to find out more

- Lane, J. (2008) *Young Children and Racial Justice.* London: National Children's Bureau.
- Lindon, J. (2010) *Reflective Practice and Early Years Professionalism: Linking Theory and Practice.* London: Hodder Arnold.
- Lindon, J. and Lindon, L. (2012) *Leadership and Early Years Professionalism: Linking Theory and Practice.* London: Hodder Arnold.
- **www.equalityhumanrights.com**
- **www.legalservices.gov.uk** – download leaflets on equality and discrimination.

Using skills appropriately

There will always be some level of diversity within a team, even if personal identity by ethnic group membership appears to offer limited variety. One aspect to equality and diversity in the team arises from how you use individuals' knowledge and skills.

Pause for reflection

Practitioners with different professional and personal backgrounds can bring a fresh perspective, but this diversity needs to be coordinated effectively. It is not good practice if individuals are trapped inside a specialism or typecast because of particular skill or experience. Please consider the following examples:

- To what extent do you feel the way of organising is appropriate?
- If the use of the practitioner's skills is inappropriate, how would you explain your reservations to the team leader or other practitioners?
- What might be a more suitable use of this practitioner's talents?

1 Sarah's husband works for a Japanese firm and Sarah has joined him on two trips to Japan. Several Japanese families are living locally in company houses and have sent their children to the playgroup. The playgroup leader has asked Sarah to be key person for these children.

2 Alistair has a Scottish father and English mother. He has started to learn Gaelic and is keen on storytelling. Everybody else in the childminding network is monolingual. Alistair would like to offer some storytelling and songs in Gaelic for the crèche that supports network meetings.

3 Ayesha's family came originally from Trinidad. She is the only Black member of staff in the private nursery, which is in a relatively diverse neighbourhood. Ayesha feels that her room colleague expects her to have a special rapport with the three Black parents, none of whom is of Caribbean origin.

4 Pete is the only practitioner in his community nursery with any experience of working with deaf children. The manager asks Pete whether he will teach two colleagues basic signing and draw up a play programme for a profoundly deaf child who is about to join the nursery.

5 Nina spent several years in an urban children's centre and has now moved to work in a nursery class serving a rural, mainly White locality. Two colleagues suggest in a team meeting that 'Nina should lead us on the multicultural celebrations. She's done all that stuff in her old job.'

6 Greg is a talented woodworker and coaches the local under-11s football team. The leader of his holiday play scheme asks Greg to take responsibility for both of these activities during the summer programme. The same request has been made for the past two years.

Equal status for team members

Diversity may arise within a team because of different professional backgrounds or job roles. Teamwork and equality practice can be undermined if a differential status has been allowed to develop between staff members.

Specialist support workers, often employed for individual disabled children, need to feel and to be treated as full colleagues in a team. Practitioners in these vital roles are sometimes working with 'assistant' titles, such as Support Learning Assistant or Specialist Teaching Assistant. Titles matter less than equality of status and professional respect, but the word can be symbolic. SLAs or STAs will feel treated as lowly assistants if they are not invited to full team meetings. The wording and reality of their job descriptions should stress their work as crucial to ensure inclusion of a child within the nursery or school setting. The result can be non-inclusive if the emphasis is more on one-to-one support of a child, with the sense that child and assistant are a unit separate from everyone else.

In schools, it is very often a different group of people, not teachers, who take responsibility for break and lunchtimes in the playground, or inside on wet-weather days.

- The supervisors, or whatever their title may be, need to be fully involved in developing and reviewing a whole-school behaviour policy.
- Children whose disabilities affect their behaviour will be out in the playground, not necessarily accompanied by a support practitioner. Playground supervisors need to be fully informed about current strategies to support such children. They also need to know about practical issues of continence for some children, or emergency medication.

Finding out more

The idea of mirroring is described by Bill Rogers as part of guiding school-age children towards more positive patterns of behaviour. See, for example, Rogers, B. (ed) (2004) *How to Manage Challenging Behaviour*. London: Paul Chapman Publishing.

Safeguarding children

Increased awareness of child abuse has complicated the issues around male practitioners. Some teams and local authorities have developed rules limiting the care responsibilities of male practitioners. When challenged, some teams or advisors have resolved the issue by applying these inappropriate rules to all practitioners. Some decision makers have been resistant, although not openly, to employing men in childcare at all. Such an approach is ineffective for child protection, discriminatory towards men and the no-touch policies are potentially damaging for young children (see also page 100).

A major misunderstanding arises from the inaccurate claim that 'Most abusers are male.' Men predominate in sexual abuse but not in physical abuse, neglect or the emotional abuse of children. Some sexual abuse is also perpetrated by females. Women can be cruel to children and neglectful of their needs, so banning men is no way to deal with child protection in early years. All settings need clear procedures for taking on paid employees and volunteers, and a working atmosphere in which children, parents and practitioners feel able to raise any concerns (Lindon, 2012).

Scenario

At Falcon Square after-school club, Daniel, the team leader, and five-year-old Lucy are sitting on a garden bench when she asks, 'What's a perv?' Daniel replies, 'I'll answer your question, Lucy. But first can you tell me what made you ask?' Lucy says willingly, 'My grandad says that blokes must be pervs if they want to work with little children.'

Daniel is faced with a tricky situation, but decides that Lucy's question deserves an answer. He replies, 'Well, that word is used for people who want to hurt children. I want to be here with you all because I really enjoy working in a club. Maybe I need to have a chat with your mum and dad. I'm sad to think that anyone in your family might be worried.'

Daniel decides that he needs to approach Lucy's parents about the conversation and will raise the issue with the rest of the team to let them all know how he handled the situation.

Questions

1 Have you faced a similar situation?
2 Might there be any further issues to resolve when Daniel explains the incident to his colleagues?

If you want to find out more

- ACAS (2010) *Rights at Work: Equality and Discrimination,* **www.acas.org.uk/ media/pdf/a/3/Equality___discrimination(RAW)_OCTOBER_2010.pdf**
- Lindon, J. (2012) *Safeguarding Children 0–8 Years.* London: Hodder Education.
- Lindon, J. and Lindon, L. (2012) *Leadership and Early Years Professionalism.* London: Hodder Education. (Chapter 1 in particular.)
- Owen, C. (2003) *Men's Work: Changing the Gender Mix of the Childcare and Early Years Workforce.* London: Policy Paper 6, Daycare Trust, **www.koordination-maennerinkitas.de/uploads/media/Owen-Charlie-Men_s-Work_02.pdf**
- Rolfe, H. (2005) *Men in Childcare,* Occupational Segregation Working Paper Series No 35, Equal Opportunities Commission (now Equality and Human Rights Commission, **www.equalityhumanrights.com**

Professional behaviour and social learning

Everyone brings to adulthood the results of learning within their own childhood. Professionalism is about addressing when you need to be flexible in your habits of language and behaviour, and also in understanding those of your colleagues. You cannot know everything, nor can you manage daily professional life, frozen in anxiety about unintentionally giving offence. Your responsibility is to learn more, within the knowledge that many social and cultural traditions change over time. Similar issues are raised in the context of partnership in Chapter 10.

Patterns of communication

Broad patterns of verbal and non-verbal communication are laid down in childhood, as children learn their family way. Individual families are affected by the ethnic group and cultural background of the adults, but there is usually a great deal of variation within any group. In open discussion, individuals may fairly counter with 'We never did that in my family.' Any examples in this section, or other parts of the book, are possibilities and not firm predictions.

Same language – different use of words

You and your colleague can both be fluent in one language, yet use the same words to convey a different meaning. I was initially taken aback by a friend from Guyana (one of the mainland South American Caribbean countries). My friend would remark, 'You lie!' when I said something that surprised her. It took me more than one uneasy conversation to realise she was not suggesting what I said was untrue. Her words were the equivalent of 'You're kidding me!' or 'You don't say!' However, I had other friends whose country of origin was Guyana but who did not use that phrase. There are many different ethnic and cultural traditions in Guyana and I never worked out whether my friend's phrase arose from her cultural group. It could have been exclusive to her family, as indeed I use phrases that are particular to my own family upbringing.

Partnership with parents and families

Early years, school and out-of-school practitioners need to aim for a friendly relationship with parents, but it is still a professional relationship. The overall aim of a working partnership fits well with equality practice. You have a continuing obligation to deal with all the parents in an even-handed way. There will be differences between you and individual parents, and some sources of diversity may feel like a wide gap.

Professional practice is to recognise and deal with feelings of unease or confusion that may block partnership. One way to dissolve the blocks will be to extend your knowledge and be willing to discuss issues. This chapter covers some situations in which agreement or compromise may be difficult. An equality policy is not a value-free zone. This chapter, like other parts of the book, offers examples where practitioners have to be clear about the priorities underpinning their practice.

The main sections of this chapter cover:
● first impressions
● diversity within family life
● continuing partnership.

First impressions

All early years, school and playwork practitioners need to consider how they welcome prospective users of the service. The early contacts and first impressions are important and these are only partly created through communication between the adults. Good practice in creating an inclusive environment for children will show positive attitudes to parents through resources and events on the day they first visit.

Welcome and open communication

Good partnership is led through communication. From the beginning of your working relationship it is important to show that you would genuinely like to get to know families and their children. You develop familiarity with each other over time. Of course, you are not obligated to find out everything in the first meeting. Continued partnership is supported by opportunities for relaxed conversation, just chatting.

Families will realise that you are genuinely interested in them and their children without wishing to interfere in family life. Be prepared to share some personal

Figure 10.1 Partnership recognises the importance of children's family

information in return. If you are expressing an interest in a parent's country of origin, it is perfectly reasonable that they ask, and you answer, similar questions about where you spent your childhood. If any conversations raise issues of boundaries between professional and personal life, be prepared to reflect on how to draw limits, and discuss these with colleagues or an advisor.

There will always be some sources of diversity within practitioner and parent groups, and some of those sources of group identity may not be shared. For example, it is very often the case that an entire nursery team is female; yet some of the parents closely involved with their children's nursery life will be fathers. In neighbourhoods with significant language diversity, it is likely that some languages will be spoken by some parents but by none of the staff team. You do not have to share specific sources of personal identity in order to make friendly contact.

Considerate decisions may be made about personal ways to make a parent or family feel welcome and to ease communication.
- More group settings now are aware of being actively father friendly, and that means more than sticking up one picture of a man holding a baby.
- Some parents will have children with disabilities; some parents will themselves have a disability. Good practice in partnership responds to the individuality of

families and their needs. But parents of disabled children will not want a specialist version of partnership that treats them as different in every way.

- Perhaps no practitioner in a team has any personal experience of family life as Travellers or Gypsies, but lack of knowledge should not be a block; there are many resources on which you can draw (see page 57).

Temporary, closer partnerships within a group setting should not act in an exclusive way. Any specialist group sessions, or other form of contact, should work to help parents feel more included in the setting or service. You do not want special initiatives to highlight a set of parents as permanently different, or appearing more favoured, in comparison with other parents. Adults can be as prone to object 'It's not fair; they're getting more than us!' as their young children.

Of course, it would be unacceptable for practitioners to develop a closer, or warmer, partnership on the basis of any kind of group identity of practitioner, parent or other family carer (see the scenario on page 178). It is inevitable that you will feel more comfortable with some individual parents, and they with you. But you have a responsibility to judge priorities in your work in a professional way.

- Practitioners should not spend more time with individual parents simply because they are 'people like me' – whatever the basis for this sense of fellow-feeling.
- If you work in a diverse neighbourhood, there will be parents with whom you do not share the same ethnic identity, cultural background, language or faith. It would be poor practice for anyone to develop a different kind of relationship with parents who happen to share their own cultural background or faith.

Early visits and settling-in time

Many group settings have a pattern for contact between parents and practitioners before a child's first official day. Childminders often offer a family-home version of much of the following:

- An invitation for parents, probably with their children, to visit before taking up the offer of a place. Some nurseries offer open evenings or a tea party for 'new parents'. I would suggest rethinking this phrase, if you use it. Most parents are only 'new' to your service; they are almost certainly not new to parenting or family life.
- Many group settings offer the option of a home visit, in which the designated key person, and often a second practitioner, go to the family home for the first long conversation. Parents are often pleased to have this first real contact on their home ground. Children are often delighted to show their bedroom or garden, if they have one. Some settings offer to take photos, for instance, like a child holding their favourite soft toy. These photos are printed ready to greet a child and parents on the first time they attend the setting.
- Materials that you show to explain about your service need to be accessible for anyone. Even if you and a parent share a fluent language, it is still more effective to have visual as well as written material to show 'what goes on here'.

- It is appropriate partnership practice with parents who already use your service that you check whether they are happy for photos showing their children to be part of any brochure, album or illustrated ring-binder file that is available to legitimate visitors.

Early contact can be used appropriately to consider your resources. You might ask, 'I would really like to add to my book shelf. Could you tell me about your family language? I'd like to find suitable dual-language books.' This positive approach is different from implying to parents that their arrival will require immediate purchases with a reluctant comment like 'Now I'll be Sadaf's childminder, I suppose I'd better get some special books.' In a similar way, you are not buying jigsaws featuring disabled children just because Tyrone has joined your setting, and he had one leg amputated as a result of damage in a car accident. In some cases, though, Tyrone's arrival may make a team aware of a significant gap in resources. However, the jigsaws are for everyone, as are any dual-language books.

Sharing the care of children

Friendly partnership with parents is crucial if you are to take good care of their children. Many of the practical points explored in Chapter 6 need to emerge through open communication with parents and other family carers from the very beginning. Babies and very young children will not be able to tell you about family diet or important issues over clothing or hygiene. Even slightly older children, with spoken language, may be uneasy about appearing to disagree with what a practitioner is about to do with or for them.

You need to create an atmosphere that leads parents to feel confident you really want to know and understand. Your first contacts with any individual parent should be a time when you are as concerned to hear about their child as you are to explain the way you work in your childminding practice, nursery or after-school club. Partnership needs to recognise situations that call for more specific questions. It is important to be honest if you do not know what a child is likely to need, or if you do not understand what a parent has just told you about care routines. Do not be uneasy about starting another conversation with 'I'm really not sure what makes meat halal. And if we can't find the right kind of butcher, what would you rather we did?' It is far better that you struggle with mild awkwardness now than take an option that will create avoidable annoyance to this family – or significant embarrassment for you, or your colleagues, in the future.

Parents of children with a disability have many concerns and questions in common with all families: Will their child be safe and genuinely liked by staff? Will he make friends? What will happen if she wets herself? However, if children have a disability, it is professional to have a proper discussion around some special issues.
- You need to know about this child's individual needs. It does not matter if you have previously worked with children with this disability or health condition; you still have to understand fully how Shireen's epilepsy affects her or the consequences of hemiplegia for Leroy.

- Approach the conversation with honesty, not pretending that the child is 'just like all the others' but avoiding a focus on 'difficulties'. It is the difference between the courteous question, 'What should I know about Monica's diet?' and the blunt statement, 'I see Monica's diabetic; I suppose there'll be problems about food.' The second phrase is as unacceptable as saying to Omar's parents, 'This business about Ramadan; it's bound to be difficult with the fasting.'
- You need to understand fully about health issues: any regular medication; whether children are vulnerable to infection; how to recognise an emergency for this child and what to do.
- A child's key person in a nursery will lead the care, but all the information must be shared effectively with anyone else who could come into contact with the child. The same applies to schools and breaktime staff. What happens if Rashida has a serious asthma attack and the playground supervisors have no idea what to do?

Families with disabled children come from the full variety of ethnic groups and cultural backgrounds. Awareness of these issues needs to coexist with equality focused on disability. Practitioners need to be aware of unchecked assumptions. For instance, Rashida's extended family lives a hundred miles away and her mother copes without family back-up. Leroy's mother is a lone parent, yet she has an active support network of family and friends. Work with children with disabilities within autistic spectrum disorder often aims to help them manage more eye contact. However, within some cultures, children are not encouraged to engage in significant eye contact with adults because it is judged to be impolite staring.

You might be thinking over whether it will be sensible to prepare the children already in your home or group for the child's arrival. Perhaps a child's disability is likely to lead to comments and questions from other children. It is dishonest to pretend that there is nothing unusual about Leroy. He needs to use a wheelchair for anything more than short walks and he may be the first child with a visible physical disability to join the nursery. You could discuss briefly with Leroy's mother what you plan to say.

It is possible that parents will not find out that their child has a specific disability until he or she has spent some time in nursery or with a childminder. Some parents may have been anxious for many months about their child's development or pattern of behaviour. But they have been told that their child will 'catch up', 'grow out of it' or that there is nothing wrong and they are worrying unnecessarily. Such parents may be relieved that their concerns have been supported and now perhaps someone will help. Other parents may have been unaware and are shocked to be told, however carefully, that all is not well with their child. A well-established partnership with the family will ease this sensitive situation.

Cultural diversity in names

For everyone, a name is part of your personal identity. It can feel anything from mildly discourteous to downright offensive if people make little effort to say your name properly, or persist in versions that you do not want to be called. Children deserve full attention and effort to say their name correctly. Partnership with parents is a vital route, especially with younger children who are less likely to say, 'Why do you keep calling me Steven?' and to stress, 'It's Se-jee-ven.'

Many of the practical issues that arise over names from a range of cultural traditions are covered by general good practice. However, these issues may not be highlighted until you encounter names unfamiliar to you.

- It is good practice to ensure that you spell and say correctly the names of all the children and their parents. The guideline of 'If in doubt, ask' sums up courteous behaviour applicable to partnership with every family.
- If a personal or family name is unfamiliar to you, and initially you find it hard to say, then make yourself a reminder note on how to pronounce it correctly. Children themselves are often happy to drill you in practice.
- In many cultures there are some names that can be given either to boys or girls. The sex of babies and toddlers is not always obvious. If you are in any doubt about names unfamiliar to you, then find out politely.
- Ensure that you write down the names of both parents, if there are two in the family. UK families do not necessarily all share the same surname, even when parents are married to each other.

The European system of naming is far from universal. Most cultural traditions give names in addition to a single personal name. But many do not include the idea that all members of a family will share one common name – the European 'surname'. Not everyone, by any means, places the personal name first. So you need to check with parents the name by which you should address a child. Some families describe this as the 'calling name'. Here are some examples but, as you might guess, there is considerable diversity within as well as between cultural traditions.

- Chinese naming systems have traditionally put the shared family name first, a generation name may follow and then a personal name. So, if Shek Gai Wai is about to join your home as a childminder, the most likely situation is that Shek is her family name, Gai indicates that she is a child in the family and Wai is her personal name. Vietnamese families follow a similar pattern.
- Hindu families place the personal name first, followed by another name such as bhai (brother) or devi (goddess). When children have a name that could be given to a boy or a girl, the second name will specify their sex. For instance, Anu Kumar (prince) Sharma is a boy, whereas Anu Kumari (princess) Patel is a girl. The last name for Hindu families is a shared family name that indicates the family's traditional status and occupation. This system led to many people having the same last name and Hindu practice is to record the father's or husband's name for extra identification.

- Sikh tradition broke with Hinduism and with the system that last names reflect the caste system. Devout Sikh families will still not use a last name. Children have a personal name, usually followed by Kaur (princess) for a girl and Singh (lion) for a boy. Surinder Kaur may also have a last name, by which all the family is known. Otherwise, Surinder's father should be called Mr Singh and her mother Mrs Kaur.
- Muslim boys are often given a personal and a religious name (one of the names of Allah). The religious name often, but not always, comes first and adult men would usually be addressed by both names. Children are called by the personal name; it would be offensive to use only a boy's religious name as his calling name. So Muhammad Hamid Sheikh has a religious first name, a personal second and Sheikh is the family name. Girls are not given a religious name, so Hamid's sister is Razia Sheikh.

Families from a variety of backgrounds may choose to change the order of names, or agree on a shared family name, out of consideration for confused practitioners or to make daily life more straightforward in the UK. Families who follow Islam do not traditionally have a shared family name. But in the UK many Muslim families use hereditary names denoting social position or religious grouping, or use the father's personal name as a surname.

Names matter

Practitioners should follow the child's and parents' wishes over how a child is known, if this name is not their full first name. Some children prefer to be called by a shortened version of their name, or they have more than one personal name and choose to be known by the second one. Certainly, practitioners should never shorten or change a child's name (or a colleague's for that matter) to avoid the small amount of effort needed to learn the proper name.

Be sensitive in your first conversations with a family. If a family has experienced discourtesy about how to say or spell their name, they may tolerate simplification for an easy life. Sometimes parents want to avoid embarrassing a practitioner who has made the mistake more than once in this conversation. You can acknowledge that a name is unfamiliar to you with comments like, 'Can I make sure that I am saying your daughter's name correctly?' Avoid any suggestion that a name is 'odd'. Neither is a child's name 'difficult'; you are finding it hard to say because of unfamiliarity.

All languages do not include the same range of sounds and some blends can be hard to pronounce, although first-language speakers will not grasp the potential difficulty in what is 'normal' to them. If you genuinely cannot manage to say a child's name accurately, then explain the situation to parents and children. Young children sometimes struggle with patterns of sound. If your name is a challenge for any children to say, then it is your choice to simplify it.

Diversity in family life

Variety in family composition cuts across ethnic and social group diversity. Partnership with parents should be based on respect for different ways to run a family and without assumptions about who is likely to be counted within any given family group. Some children are raised by their two birth parents but some will be cared for by a lone mother or father. Some grandparents have stepped in to take parental responsibility. Some families will be formed by new relationships and step-parents and step-siblings will be part of the family. Some children may have been adopted or are in a long-term foster placement.

Male family carers

There are considerably more fathers in the nursery or school grounds than was the case with previous generations. But, with a workforce that is still predominantly female, fathers say that they can still feel like the exception. Female practitioners need to be aware of their own attitudes and offer respect for male carers such as fathers.

- Watch out that you do not assume that this is a temporary arrangement and ask when the child's mother will be coming.
- Male carers may be lone parents or may be the primary carer in a two-parent family. Some families organise their time so that both parents share in taking children to and from a childminder, nursery or school.
- Communicate directly with the parent in front of you and avoid the less respectful habit of using fathers simply as a channel for sending messages back to the child's mother.
- When both parents come, avoid addressing most remarks to the mother or always asking her questions about health or routine.

If you have a mixed male–female team, some fathers may be more comfortable talking with a male practitioner. It would be appropriate to respect this preference over a settling-in period, but a male practitioner should behave in ways that enable this parent to feel more at ease with other team members. Fathers should not be directed towards a male practitioner as a matter of course, no more than parents should automatically be guided towards conversation with a team member who shares their ethnic group identity or faith.

Of course, it is important not to assume that the shape of partnership changes radically for fathers. However, it is professional to reflect on how far daily exchanges or invitations for different types of involvement are underpinned by the unspoken assumption that 'parents' actually means mothers. A special event for fathers and other male carers can help to get the ball rolling. It may be a 'Dads' day', special 'Fathers' evening' or 'Bring your dad or grandad to nursery' event. Combined social and information events can be a relaxed way for practitioners in a team to hear from male family members what they would like to do or would be willing to do if asked.

It can help to have newsletters or family noticeboards that ask for a wide variety of help and cite some specific tasks rather than a general welcome to get involved. I saw a very effective noticeboard in one primary school. It had a general message about how much the school, including the nursery, welcomed parents' involvement. Then an array of about ten photographs showed named fathers, mothers and different family members busy with different recent projects and tasks.

Gay and lesbian families

Gay and lesbian parents are a group with a great deal of individual variation, just like any social group of people. They may feel understandably under pressure or scrutiny about their sexual orientation and the negative reaction of some people to their raising children. So you may not necessarily know that an individual parent is gay or lesbian. These mothers and fathers will want to talk to you about the wide range of issues that affects children and that they share with their fellow parents. They will want you to relate to them in their social role as 'parent' to their children. Their sexuality may not arise as an issue, any more than your own sexual orientation or whether you have a current partner.

Children in gay and lesbian families do not seem to be confused about their own sex or in finding an appropriate gender identity for themselves. Children's emotional stability and well being depend on how they are treated by adults, not those adults' sexual orientation. Living in a gay or lesbian family does not appear to push children's later choices about sexual orientation one way or another. As many gay and lesbian parents point out, they were raised by a heterosexual couple.

If you are uncertain how to deal with children's comments or questions, then talk with the parent(s). They will have experience and preferences about how their family is described. Parents could be valuable in helping you decide how best to reply when one child says to another, 'You can't have two mummies' or asks, 'Is Mike your daddy's lodger?' Children can be made unhappy or feel isolated if their family situation is met with hostility or offensive amusement. In an unwelcoming local community, children may feel they have to be secretive about their family. Children are rarely comfortable keeping secrets that prevent their talking about what is important to them.

For all the changes in society, there is still a considerable amount of hostility towards people who are gay, lesbian or bisexual. Insults based on sexual orientation are part of the offensive vocabulary of many school-age children. Outright rejection is also strong in some social and cultural groups, and actively promoted by followers of some world faiths. This equality issue is another area in which you need to be clear about the prevailing values of your practice. You will not be able to please everyone and adult hostility will almost certainly be reflected in children's comments, especially by school age.

Partnership and disability

Bear in mind that some parents will themselves be disabled. In some cases they will be the disabled parent of a disabled child, but not necessarily. Good practice in partnership does not become entirely different when parents are disabled. Many of the adjustments are more generally inclusive.

It is as important that you build an individual relationship with disabled parents as with individual children who are disabled. Practitioners are sometimes told that they should not treat the child of a disabled parent as a child in need. This advice is somewhat confusing, unless the meaning is unpacked. When there is disability in the family, the situation should not be treated as nothing but 'problems'. However, children whose parents are disabled have individual needs that deserve attention – just as with the siblings of disabled children. Family life for everyone is shaped by the presence of disability, as recognised by the Children (Scotland) Act 1995, which defines children as 'in need' when anyone within the immediate family is disabled.

Scenarios

1

In St Agnes Pre-school, Suzanne does not object to being known, at least sometimes, as 'Ricky's mum' – it is a normal part of life with young children. But Suzanne objected to how Sophie, a practitioner who has now left, had sometimes referred to her as 'the one in the wheelchair'. The parish council had already installed a ramp to ease access to the hall, but Suzanne's arrival with Ricky had shown that the narrow entrance lobby also posed problems.

In the early weeks, Suzanne expressed appreciation to Michelle for her approach along the lines of 'How can we make pre-school life straightforward for you?' Suzanne simply wished to get on with the task of being a mother to Ricky. In the same conversation she raised her frustration with Sophie, who tended either to ignore her or to insist on 'helping' without first asking whether Suzanne wanted any support.

2

Parents may have learning disabilities rather than physical disabilities. The kind and extent of learning disabilities vary considerably, so it is impossible to make broad generalisations. In Clearwater nursery class, Helena is ready to offer advice and support to Marie, whose learning disabilities mean that she is uncertain how best to care for Thomas or what kind of play resources are suitable for a nearly four-year-old. Young children can be very protective towards their parents, and Thomas already notices that his mother behaves differently from other parents. Helena is aware that Thomas could become a young carer for his mother. Helena wishes to help Marie to accept support from the local family support team.

Comments

Appropriate support for disabled parents will never be a single template. You develop partnership with individual parents and families.

Are you aware of support teams or facilities in your area? Collect information on services that could be useful to parents like Suzanne or Marie.

Continuing partnership

Good practice in partnership allows for variety and offers an active respect to parents. The vast majority of parents are interested in their children, concerned about their well being and closely involved in their lives. Parents will have a different perspective from your professional outlook – they need to be focused on their own child – but otherwise you will have much in common.

Clear communication

Unless parents have specific early years professional experience, they will not necessarily grasp how 'learning through play' is an effective approach for young children. Bafflement about what you are doing and why can be shared between families of different ethnic groups and cultural background, as can pressure over literacy or numeracy. Some parents may expect the after-school club to operate as an extension of the school day. Even if you offer space and some resources for children to do their homework, club practitioners are not taking parental responsibility for the quality or accuracy of children's work.

Take another **perspective**

Unspoken assumptions can also make communication more complicated. Liz Brooker (2002) observed the experiences of families over one reception year in an urban primary school. She described how well-intentioned practice, like the class teacher's open-door approach to communication, did not work to include the Bangladeshi families. The staff did not seem to have realised how much the children learned at home, or that many parents had serious reservations about the effectiveness of school for their children.

Families from a range of cultural or national backgrounds may appreciate a more formal approach to first contacts with a setting, talking about their children or ways to raise confusions or concerns. The UK approach, especially in early years, tends to be informal, with the expectation that parents will simply approach practitioners or 'know' that they are welcome. Some parents prefer a more definite request for specific involvement, with the option, of course, of declining.

- Brooker, L. (2002) *Starting School: Young Children Learning Cultures*. Buckingham: Open University Press.

Communication to show and tell can be less straightforward when you do not share a fluent language with parents. A lack of shared language complicates communication, and even good interpreters may not fully understand the ideas that you need to have explained and to understand in your turn. However, miscommunication is still very possible when you speak a shared language. The best way forward is to offer different channels of communication and to have an open and flexible working definition of partnership. Open days or evenings can work well for some parents as a way to experience the general approach of a group setting to children's learning. Parents often appreciate seeing the rooms set up and enjoy some of the experiences in a hands-on way. Such opportunities can be well supported by straightforward explanations from practitioners about 'what your child can learn from ...'.

Adult literacy

Another approach to communication is through a family noticeboard, newsletter or other regular summary. Written material ideally needs to be in the main local languages. It will help everyone if you make generous use of visual materials to illustrate your messages. But practitioners need to recall that illiteracy, or a limited ability to read and write, is a hidden problem for many adults, across social and cultural groups. Traveller and Gypsy parents have often had disrupted schooling in their own childhood. However, a significant number of adults have developed strategies to cover their inability to read, such as 'I haven't got my glasses' or 'My wife deals with all that.' Sometimes, of course, these statements are true. A sensitive approach will benefit all parents, including those who cope with dyslexia, a disability that affects how children and adults are able to process written language.

All written material, and spoken exchanges too, need to be expressed in straightforward language.

- All professions have special words and phrases that are jargon to outsiders. Early years, school and playwork practitioners are no exception, and some degree courses have encouraged the use of academic terms.
- Considerate attention to use of words will benefit partnership as a whole. Parents who share a fluent language with you are unlikely to follow what you mean by 'gross motor development', let alone 'gender equity'. Fellow adults, working in their less fluent language, will be utterly perplexed.

- Newsletters or other written material will be done now on a word processor. It should be very easy to run off some copies in a large font size, if that will enable some parents to read the text. It would be wasteful of paper to run off every copy in that larger font, though.
- Can you offer simple audio-tape versions of newsletters or other written communication? You could involve children in setting up a comfortable corner where anyone can listen to the tape, at the same time as looking at written, and illustrated, material.

Partnership over disability

Any setting or service has to find a suitable middle course between treating the presence of disabled or sick children as a problem, about which other parents should be 'warned', and an equally inappropriate stance of 'It doesn't make any difference at all.' You may have judged it sensible to prepare the children to welcome a child. If so, then be ready for parents who ask questions because their children have said, 'Tyrone lost his leg, you know' or 'We've got to help Debbie, 'cos she's got "tism".'

Be ready to answer factual questions from family members about 'Is it catching?' or 'Are you sure you'll still have enough attention for all the other children?' Avoid assuming parents are making an unreasonable fuss, unless their persistence or language supports an interpretation that they are prejudiced about disability. The presence of a disabled or sick child should not trigger a stream of letters home to all parents. However, there may be occasions when a letter is appropriate.

For example, Tom's disability involves significant behavioural or emotional difficulties. He had a prolonged outburst today that distressed and frightened other children. You should think seriously about writing to parents under such circumstances, otherwise the local grapevine will buzz and some parents will fairly ask why they had to pick up details from their own children. It would be courteous to let Tom's parent know that the letter will be sent. If this incident is not the first, you might also need to reflect whether you can genuinely meet Tom's needs without further support for your setting.

Take another **perspective**

Within the parent group, as with colleagues in a team, there will be a broad variation in emotions, as well as knowledge, about disability and serious health conditions. There are many appropriate options between the two extremes of a slick sentimentality about disabled children ('so brave') and a grim hopelessness ('so terrible'). The wide range of emotions experienced by parents of disabled or very sick children can better be understood by reading some of the books suggested on page 167, as well as, of course, by listening to parents who wish to talk.

The other source of mixed feelings, for which practitioners need to be prepared, is the concern felt by colleagues or parents who are themselves pregnant or whose partner is expecting a baby. Usual anxieties about the well being of your baby are heightened by an awareness of what can happen, however unlikely that may be statistically. I became personally aware of this issue through working with the staff of a unit for profoundly disabled children over the months I was pregnant with my daughter. Practitioners and fellow parents can care very much about individual disabled children, yet not wish for their experiences to be repeated for the adult's unborn child.

Explanation of values in practice

You start the process of explaining equality within the early days of partnership. Some questions, or challenges, may arise from parents at that early point. Some comments may be voiced later. Taking the example of equality over gender, some parents will share your views and be pleased to give active support for what you do. Some parents may appreciate a chance to express their frustrations, because they have been trying to extend a son or daughter's interests, against opposition from a partner or relative. However, some parents or other family carers will disagree with gender equality in practice, for reasons related to cultural or faith traditions. Some of these parents will be White UK families, certainly not all from groups classified as minority ethnic.

You share with parents what happens in your service; you are not telling them what they have to do in their own family. Perhaps in Annop's home (or Wai-yung's or Benjie's for that matter) it is usual that his mother and sisters do all the domestic tasks. The boys may find it odd in nursery or your home that you expect them to do up their own coat and help at tidy-up time. Friendly conversation with a child's parent can help practitioners to understand the gap between the family pattern and nursery, club or your home as a childminder. With your patience and encouraging invitation, it is very likely that children will choose to be like their peers and follow 'what we do here'. Their behaviour is unlikely to change at home while they have 'their people' serving them.

Take another perspective

Read through the following examples and consider how you might reply if a parent said this to you. You could compare ideas with a colleague or fellow student.

1. 'It says in your brochure something about equal opportunities and gender. What exactly does that mean?'

2. 'I don't want you to let my son do this needlework stuff. He's a boy; he should be playing with cars and trains, not doing embroidery. Are you trying to turn them into wimps?'

3. 'Tasha's gran has been going on about your clambering frame. She has a thing about girls falling on their privates; she stopped my wife climbing when she was young. Is it dangerous?'

origins of May Day celebrations, how to do some country dancing or make a traditional Lancashire hot pot. Many people will have very little idea.

- Avoid assuming that Saira's father will not want to join a rota of parents who come in to support craft activities needing careful supervision. Perhaps you hesitate with, 'It'll be too difficult – what with his withered hand.' Suitable equality practice is to include Owen in the invitation and be ready if he wants to raise practical issues about his chosen involvement.

- Chris's parents may be knowledgeable about thalassaemia, because of their son's condition, but they are unlikely to want to be pigeon-holed as the people who always speak up about any disability or health issue. Perhaps Chris's father is itching to mend and extend your inadequate book shelves, but he does not wish to seem 'pushy'.

Personal histories

Any family that has moved country or continent within recent generations could be described as having a country of origin as well as their current roots. Some families classified as 'Black Minority Ethnic' are of recent arrival in the UK, but some have lived here for many years, in some cases for generations. There will always be variety in how families view themselves, and practitioners need to be aware of their unchecked assumptions. It is important, and courteous, that you do not make assumptions about children's allegiances. For instance, you should ask a general question of a mixed group such as 'Has anyone any connections with India?' rather than homing in on one child with 'India's your country, isn't it, Rajiv?'

Pause for reflection

Part of all children's personal identity is their family history. You could develop a project on family timelines. Whatever the extent of ethnic group diversity in your local community, you will be able to explore whether local families have moved around the country, or between countries. Several considerations will help you to make this project a positive experience.

- Talk with parents about the plans for the project and reassure them, if necessary, that you are not delving into their family history out of nosiness.

- Make sure that each family's timeline is treated with equal interest and respect. Families who have lived in the area for generations are as interesting as those who have family origins in other countries.

- The families with strong local roots may take you towards an exploration of history for children. For instance, 'What was happening at the same time that Sara's great-grandparents were running the farm?' or 'Hamish's family lived here when the shipbuilding yards were still open.'

- Families who have moved country recently, or in past generations, may be a direct way to make sense of geography for children, as may the experience of Traveller and Gypsy families.
- Be aware and sensitive about refugee families whose moves will not have been a matter of choice, but forced by war and other political disruptions.

Dealing with misunderstanding or disagreement

There will always be some potential imbalance between practitioners and parents, or other family carers. Childminders and practitioners in group settings are responsible for following the policies that underpin good professional practice. No practitioner can flex on key values, however strongly a parent might feel to the contrary. Part of good practice, as a sole practitioner like a childminder, as well as a team member, is to know what is negotiable with parents and what is not. You will have a clear policy over discipline. Good practice in partnership does not mean you ever agree to handle a child's behaviour in a way that is emotionally or physically harsh. It does not matter how clearly parents give you permission to hit their children, nor whether they support this tactic by faith or cultural tradition.

Scenario

Over the last year Clearwater nursery class have been looking closely at their approach to girls and boys through the daily play activities. The rethink has been part of reflection for the whole school team led by Philip, the new head teacher. Within the nursery, the team decided to take a more active line in encouraging play to blur some children's firm ideas about what was girls' and boys' play, as well as what mummies and daddies usually did.

Philip has looked at the possibilities within the whole school staff team (mainly female) to promote diversity through adult role models. There have been active efforts to show that male practitioners can get involved in nursery opportunities like cooking and dressing up. They also worked to show the less enthusiastic boys that men enjoy reading and writing. The team has also looked at female practitioners, physically active play and how playground supervisors deal with games that have often been labelled as 'rough' and stopped. The team rewrote the school equality policy with more emphasis on gender, and have displayed the main ideas, with photographs of recent projects with the children in the nursery and main section of the school.

Over the next fortnight several parents asked to speak with Susan or Helena in the nursery. Two fathers do not think their sons should put on the wraps or the favourite feather boa from the extended dressing-up materials. A couple of parents are concerned that children are 'being made' to do activities more suitable for the opposite sex. One mother refers to the Clearwater policy on partnership and the commitment to respect families' religious and cultural traditions. Similar concerns are being raised by some parents whose children are in the primary school, although other families are very positive.

Questions

1 What are the main issues that Philip and his team face with this dilemma? With hindsight, could they have approached their new policy and practice in a different or better way?

2 Encouraging children to step across firm sex-role boundaries can worry families from a range of cultural or religious backgrounds. Have you faced a similar dilemma in your own centre?

....

A vital element in partnership will always be to explain to parents at the first meeting – through conversation and written material about your service – how some aspects of practice are non-negotiable. Further conversation will be necessary if events lead to potential disagreement. When parents and practitioners hold incompatible views with equal conviction, a discussion will not be easy but can be possible. Honesty, tact and respect for views that you do not share may help to bring about a working acceptance or compromise in most circumstances. If parents continue to ask that you meet requirements that are contrary to key values of your service, then regrettably there may have to be a parting of the ways. (See the example on page 104.)

It is crucial that you do not immediately assume that a parent is about to argue or be awkward. When parents voice concerns or questions, they are certainly not always cross. But a dismissive response to their first comment can tip even a courteous parent towards a sharp reply. You will experience individual differences in style from parents. Some differences may be shaped by that person's cultural background; some may be more about temperament.

- Some parents may find it hard to express a concern without cranking up the volume or using gestures that you feel to be excessive. Some cultural traditions are more forthright than others. It would be unprofessional to label a more lively style than your own as 'aggressive' or 'threatening'.
- Some parents will have trouble coming to the point. For personal or cultural reasons, they may be very concerned that they do not appear rude or unappreciative. They still have concerns that should be heard. You may need to look and listen beyond comments such as 'I don't want you to feel I'm making a fuss ...'. You need to hear the unspoken 'but ...' and invite the mother, father or grandparent to say more.
- The best approach will always be to listen to what a parent wishes to say to you. Ask open-ended questions so you can understand the key issues for this parent. Useful questions are often started with 'What ...?' or 'How ...?' or the request, 'Can you tell me more, please? I'm not quite clear what you don't like about ...'.
- Once you have listened and understood, you can make a more appropriate response and that may include saying, 'Thank you for telling me about this. I need to think over what you've said [or talk with my colleagues]. I'll get back to you tomorrow [or another time in the near future].'

A professional approach to partnership means that you reflect on how far it is appropriate to adjust your behaviour in order to acknowledge the family cultural tradition. Sometimes you will appreciate opportunities to discuss choices in a situation with colleagues, a local advisor or network supporter.

It is professional to modify your preferred approach to using physical contact, how close you stand to another person or your comfortable level of eye contact, if your habits are making someone else feel less at ease.

It is also appropriate to use less informal modes of address, if parents or family carers do not wish to be called by their personal name. (Schools are usually more formal than early years or out-of-school provision.) However, be aware that in any kind of communication, it can indicate differential status if one person is always known as Mr or Mrs Johnson and someone else is always addressed as Jane.

Scenario

At Falcon Square after-school club, a mother whose son has just started takes Daniel to one side and says, 'I would have thought twice if I'd known you had a Muslim fundamentalist working here.' Daniel is genuinely perplexed and asks, 'Who is it you're talking about?' The mother gestures towards Josie, who was raised as Muslim but has only recently started to wear a close-fitting headscarf. She has married Quasim, who is happier if she covers her hair outside the home. Daniel replies, 'That's Josie. I think she was on holiday when you visited with Sean. Josie wears her headscarf as part of her faith but that doesn't make her extremist. Is that what you mean by "fundamentalist"?'

Daniel will need to judge whether Sean's mother wants, or needs, further conversation and whether Josie could usefully be part of that discussion. However, it would not be at all appropriate to agree to any request that Sean should have little to do with Josie. Nor would it be right to agree that Shamima or Gayatri, both from Muslim families, are only in contact with Josie. The same principle would hold in an early years setting where choices would be made about a key person for children.

Questions

1 Recent events globally and in the UK have increased the ease with which some people link Islam with extremism. How have you dealt, or would you deal, with similar comments in your own practice?

2 Effective partnership with parents may first need reflection in the team. Perhaps some practitioners are themselves swift to believe that some signs of religious faith, like a headscarf, are evidence of hard-line views, whereas the crucifix worn by a Christian colleague is 'just a cross on a chain'.

When females are judged inferior

Discussion in this chapter and elsewhere in the book has recognised that gender equality applies to men as well as women. A man can feel very isolated as a father in an otherwise all-mothers drop-in or the 'token male' in an all-female team. Some communities have developed in ways that are hostile to men as fathers or any other role. This section now addresses the situation that can arise because some ethnic groups and cultural traditions place considerably less value on females – girls and women – than on males.

Sometimes such a tradition is supported by interpretations from a world faith. In case any readers are leaping to conclusions, the faith in question is not inevitably Islam and all Muslims do not interpret the Qur'an in ways that severely limit female daily life. Some sects within Christianity and Judaism require women to remain in a subservient role. But there is not always a religious connection. Some Gypsy and Traveller communities encourage behaviour towards females that is hard for outsiders to interpret other than as discourtesy. In some groups, though not all, it is usual for males to refuse to answer a woman until more than one time of asking. Practitioners need to understand patterns of behaviour from young boys but, of course, they may also experience communication that feels discourteous from fathers.

Female professionals within equality practice have struggled with the dilemma of showing respect to traditions whose followers decline to show active respect in return. To date, the most usual way of resolving the dilemma has been to weigh respect for ethnic group, cultural tradition or faith as more important than gender issues. People have also been the most anxious about accusations of being 'racist', and the easiest way out has been to skate over these issues. This situation is sensitive and littered with interpersonal potholes. But circumstances are not resolved by ignoring them, so I offer my views in the following section. Please read it more than once and use the ideas to support personal reflection and discussion in a team.

A respectful way of dealing with disrespect

There are limits to how far women should be expected to travel along the road of allegedly 'different yet equal'. Nor are such situations exclusively about gender; they are about right of respect for the cultural traditions of women who have learned they are of equal significance with men.

- It is appropriate professional effort that you seek to identify the underpinning reason for what feels like discourtesy to you. Your responsibility is to understand the sources of behaviour, to realise that at one level the words and actions are not directed at you personally.
- This realisation may help you stop searching for what you have done or said that appears to have annoyed this father or other male family member – or whatever other emotion you are using in a struggle for interpretation.
- At another level, this male reaction is disrespectful because it is utterly impersonal. Female practitioners can receive a standard pattern of response, regardless of their own behaviour and professional skills.
- Equality practice would direct you to challenge such a pattern if it were on the basis of skin colour or another ethnic group marker. The behaviour is no more acceptable on the basis of gender.

Suppose you face a continuing situation where a male family member of a child in your care seems to feel he is justified in telling you, as a female, what is to be done with his child (or grandchild). The communication is not a conversation; it is a list of orders. Perhaps you are interrupted on a regular basis by a father who is not prepared to wait if you are talking with another woman. Perhaps a child's male family carer ignores you (and you are sure he is not deaf), or pointedly waits to reply until you have asked courteously several times to speak with him.

You allow generous time to establish partnership with families, as well as showing a consistent model of what is regarded as courtesy in your service or setting. Then it is appropriate to address what you observe to be happening on a regular basis. You might say with a level, yet firm, tone of voice:

- 'I appreciate that you prefer talking with Harry. However, I am the team leader of this nursery and on issues such as ... it is appropriate that you talk with me. If you prefer, Harry can be part of that discussion, but I will lead the meeting and I will make the final decision.'
- 'Thank you for letting me know you want to have a word. I will be with you as soon as I have finished talking with Donna's mother.' ... 'Mr Johnson, I will be able to listen to you when I have finished with Mrs Kelly.' ... 'Mr Johnson, please do not interrupt us again.'
- 'Thank you for letting me know these important details about your son's care. I need to talk with his key person and then I'd like to get back to you.' ... 'I have heard what you would prefer and we discuss such issues in the team. I am not able simply to say "yes" to what you want.'

If the working relationship becomes tense and very awkward, you may ask for a meeting to discuss the situation. You need to approach the situation as a problem to be resolved and not as a matter of fault-finding. It may help to have a colleague also present, although you need to weigh up whether that will seem too formal or an attempt to 'outnumber'. Hold to an assertive approach with statements such as:

- 'I understand that you feel it is acceptable to tell me that I "must do" something – like yesterday when ... . However, I experience your words and gestures as discourteous to me.'
- 'I realise that you feel it is quite all right to ignore me until I have spoken at least three times to you. I wish to show respect for your cultural tradition, but I feel placed in an impossible position. In my cultural tradition, your behaviour would give a clear message of discourtesy. I want to try to find some way out of this that leaves us both reasonably comfortable.'
- 'I wish to show respect for your cultural tradition [faith], but not to the point where I feel disrespected just because I am a woman and you are a man. This situation is giving me problems around ... and I would like to find a way through.'

Bear in mind that many adults, from a wide range of social and cultural backgrounds, have not had much experience in taking an assertive, rather than aggressive, approach, or of constructive approaches to conflict resolution. This kind of approach is characterised by statements that are honest about your own feelings, show respect for the other person's perspective and yet make it clear that you are not content for matters to carry on in the same way (see the examples on page 218). The aim of this kind of discussion is to reach an easier pattern of interaction. You are very unlikely to change deep-rooted habits. Just be pleased if family members will adjust their behaviour enough to make daily conversation more constructive.

Supporting parents

When families experience a supportive partnership, they may well ask you for advice or guidance for further information. Part of continued professional development is for you to extend your knowledge but just as much your skills of how to find more information. Nevertheless, it is important to be aware of boundaries to partnership.

- Confident and experienced practitioners may need to be careful not to take over from families. You offer support; you do not step into the parent's role.
- You can share your knowledge of local support organisations or sources that are more national, but it is the family's choice what they follow up and what decisions they make.
- It can be valuable for you to keep a folder of local information, especially in a group setting. But ensure that you update it regularly. The message to families also needs to be clear between information you provide about support agencies or organisations and active recommendation.
- Some families – for example, refugee and asylum-seeker families – may need accurate legal advice. You may be able to suggest reliable sources of information, but be clear about the limits to your expertise.

A valuable role in partnership can be to put families in contact with other professionals who could offer expertise – for instance, to disabled children and their families. Some agencies will already be involved with a family and you will be informed through communicative partnership with parents. Be ready to learn from physiotherapists or speech therapists, so that you understand the work being done with children and can help where appropriate. However, a child's special needs may become clear during the time of your involvement, or it may be you who first raises concerns. Whatever the pattern of your involvement, it is important that talking with other professionals is never seen as more valuable than talking with children and their parents.

Of necessity, many parents become relative experts in their child's disability or health condition. If you make time to talk with and listen to them, you will extend your knowledge in general and, very important, you will understand far more about what this disability or health condition means for this individual child and family. However, not all parents of disabled children are experts, or feel as if they are.

- Good practice will be to have conversations with parents in which you give time and attention to learn from them, but also share what you know.
- Show your willingness to support parents in finding out more, either about their own child's individual needs or about the condition in general.
- Do not assume that parents will have heard about a relevant support organisation. Some parents manage with very little support or information, until they make contact with an early years setting.

You may also be a much-appreciated support for parents who are trying to weigh up advice from different sources, some of which may not be compatible. The professionals involved with a family are supposed to work cooperatively, but some parents find themselves dealing with different sources of information and firm views about how best to help their child. Some professionals are empathetic and supportive, others have a limited idea of ordinary life with a disabled child (or more than one disabled child) and the practicalities of juggling different priorities, including the needs of siblings.

Figure 10.3 Some parents appreciate special sessions

If you want to find out more

- Contact a Family – information and will try to link up families for support even when children have rare syndromes, **www.cafamily.org.uk** (accessed 31 July 2011).
- Dickins, M., with Denziloe, J. (2003) *All Together: How to Create Inclusive Services for Disabled Children and their Families.* London: National Children's Bureau.
- Disabled Parents Network, **www.disabledparentsnetwork.org.uk** (accessed 31 July 2011).
- Family Lives – advice and information to anyone supporting a child, **http://familylives.org.uk** (accessed 31 July 2011).
- Family Rights Group – advice for families involved with social services, **www.frg.org.uk** (accessed 31 July 2011).
- Fatherhood Institute – national information centre about fatherhood, **www.fatherhoodinstitute.org** (accessed 31 July 2011).
- Kahn, T. (2005) *Fathers' Involvement in Early Years Settings: Findings From Research,* **www.pre-school.org.uk** (accessed 31 July 2011).
- Lindon, J. (2009) *Parents as Partners: Positive Relationships in the Early Years.* London: Practical Pre-School Books.
- Lindon, J. (2010) *The Key Person Approach: Positive Relationships in the Early Years.* London: Practical Pre-School Books.
- Lindon, J. and Lindon, L. (2007) *Mastering Counselling Skills: Information, Help and Advice in the Caring Services.* Basingstoke: Macmillan.
- Olsen, R. and Tyers, H. (2004) *Supporting Disabled Adults as Parents,* **www.jrf.org.uk/publications/supporting-disabled-adults-parents** (accessed 31 July 2011).
- Pink Parents – focus on gay and lesbian parents, **www.pinkparents.org.uk** (accessed 31 July 2011).

Index